Dimitrii Pavlovich Sokolov

A Manual of the Orthodox Church's Divine Services

Dimitrii Pavlovich Sokolov

A Manual of the Orthodox Church's Divine Services

ISBN/EAN: 9783743335578

Manufactured in Europe, USA, Canada, Australia, Japa

Cover: Foto ©Lupo / pixelio.de

Manufactured and distributed by brebook publishing software (www.brebook.com)

Dimitrii Pavlovich Sokolov

A Manual of the Orthodox Church's Divine Services

OF

THE ORTHODOX CHURCH'S

DIVINE SERVICES.

COMPILED BY

ARCH-PRIEST D. SOKOLOF.

Translated from the Russian.

WYNKOOP HALLENBECK CRAWFORD CO.,
PRINTERS,
NEW YORK AND ALBANY.
. 1899.

Plan of a Russian Orthodox Church of the most usual type.

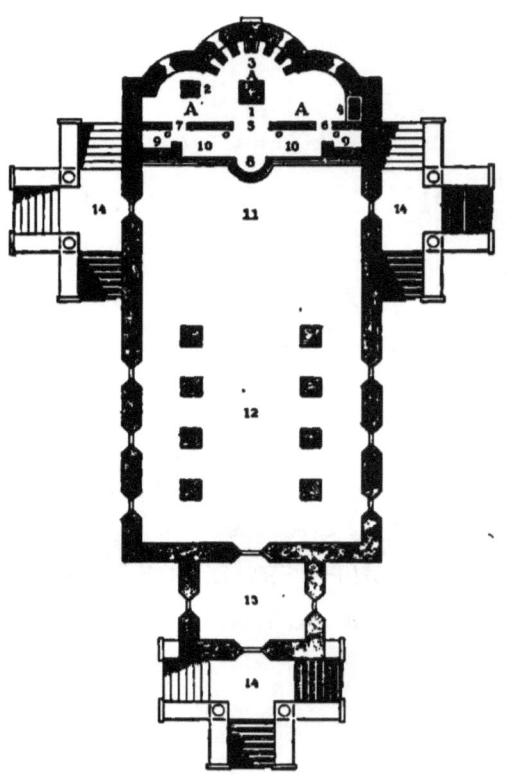

- A. The Sanctuary.
- 0. The Ikonostas (Screen).
- 1. The Altar.
- 2. The Table of Oblations.
- 3. The Bema (High Place).
- 4. The Vestry.
- 5. The Royal Gates.
- 6. The South Door.
- 7. The North Door.
- 8. The Ambo.
- 9. The Cleros (Choirs).
- 10. The Solcas.
- 11. The Nave, or Body of the church.
- 12. The Vestibule.
- 13. The Bell-tower.
- 14. The Porches.

A MANUAL

OF

The Orthodox Church's Divine Services.

Compiled by D. SOKOLOF, Arch-priest.

PRELIMINARY NOTIONS.

The Nature of Divine Service.— By "Divine Service" the Orthodox Christian Church means a series of prayers, recited or sung in a given order, with certain ceremonies, by means of which prayers Orthodox Christians glorify God and His Saints, express their thanks and prefer their petitions, and through the performance of which they receive from God mercies and the grace of the Holy Ghost.

Divine service is *private* or *domestic* when it is performed in private by one or several persons; it is *public* when it is performed in the name of the whole Church, or of a community of Christians, by persons thereto instituted. The prayers used in public worship are divided into two categories: those for *permanent* services, *i. e.* services performed daily for the benefit of all Christians, and those for *occasional* services, *i. e.* services which are performed only on certain occasions, according to the special needs of the faithful, and therefore called *treba*, a word which, translated, means "need."

The Origin of Divine Service.—Divine service made its appearance on earth simultaneously with man. The goodness and almightiness of the Lord impel men to glorify and thank Him; the consciousness of their wants prompts them to address their petitions to Him. And as man consists of both body and soul, most closely united, therefore prayer is expressed in words and accompanied by certain motions of the body, and, *vice-versa*, external objects arouse a prayerful inclination in man. In this way private worship originated and developed, varied as to prayers and rites.

But men came together and formed communities, and this gave rise to uniform prayers for all the members of one community, and for these common prayers there were gradually appointed: place, time, order of services and persons to perform them. In this way, as human society became organized, public worship also developed.

In Old Testament times, previous to Moses, divine service was of the private, domestic type. The paterfamilias — the patriarch—on behalf of his entire family or kin (tribe), selected the place, appointed the time and laid down the order of prayer. Even then certain customs already began to harden into rules which the patriarchs themselves observed, following their fathers' example. But since Moses' time, the Israelites had a public worship, instituted by God Himself, with temple, priests and rites. Jesus Christ, the founder and the Head of the Christian Church, while Himself complying with all the regulations of Jewish worship, did not give to His disciples any definite ritual. But He instituted the Sacraments, commanded His disciples to preach the Gospel, taught them how to pray, promised to be present in the gatherings of Christians assembled in His name, and thereby laid the foundation of His Church's public worship. Thus it was that, immediately after Christ's ascension to Heaven, a certain order of public worship gradually began to develop in the Christian community. In the Apostles' lifetime already, certain holy persons were consecrated, certain places were appointed for divine service, and a ritual was instituted for those offices during which the Sacraments of Baptism and the Eucharist are administered; furthermore the principal rites were devised to accompany the celebration of the other Sacraments, even to the appointing of the times for common prayer, certain feast-days and fasts. The persecutions which the Christians suffered during the first three centuries hindered them from composing an entire ritual for public worship and making it uniform for all Christians; such a ritual was fully developed and finally established only when Christianity was proclaimed the ruling religion of the Roman Empire.

External Signs used in Divine Service.— Several of the external signs of prayer are common to all men; such are: inclinations of the body, as low as the waist or all the way to the ground,—kneeling,—bowing of the head,—lifting up of the hands. All these gestures express devotion to God, humility, repentance, supplication for mercy, gratitude and reverence.

But, apart from these universal expressions of a prayerful feeling, Orthodox Christians, when praying, use a sign which belongs exclusively to them: *the sign of the cross*. This sign, according to oldest custom, we make in the following manner: the thumb, the index and the middle finger of the right hand we join together, while we bend down the third and the little fingers till they touch the palm of the hand. Having disposed the fingers after this fashion, we touch with them first the brow, then the breast, and after that first the right shoulder and then the left, thus making on our persons the sign of the cross. By this sign we express our faith in all the things which Christ the Savior taught us and did for us: by joining the three fingers, we express our faith in the Most Holy Trinity, consubstantial and undivided; by the two fingers bent to the palm of the hand we express our belief in the descent to earth of the Son of God, and in His having assumed humanity without divesting Himself of His divinity, thus uniting both natures in Himself, the divine and the human. By touching our brow, breast and shoulders, we express our belief that the Triune God hath sanctified our thoughts, feelings, desires and acts; lastly, by making on our persons the sign of the cross, we express our belief that Christ hath sanctified our soul and saved us by His sufferings on the cross.

THE CHRISTIAN TEMPLE.

Names of the various Temples and their Origin.

We give the name of *Temple* or *House of God* to a building specially consecrated to God, or to a separate part of a building so consecrated, where Christians assemble to offer up to God their common prayers, and to receive from Him His grace through the holy Sacraments. Because the totality of Christians taken together forms The Church, therefore the buildings in which they assemble for common prayer are likewise called *churches*.

Every church is consecrated to God and sanctified in the name of the Most Holy Trinity, and is therefore entitled "a temple or church of God." But apart from this general designation, each church has its own particular appellation, such as: " Church of the Holy Trinity " " of the Resurrection of Christ " " of the Holy Apostles, Peter and Paul;" " of the Assumption of the Most Holy Mother of God " " of St. Andrew the First-called " " of Bishop Nicholas Thaumaturgus." Special names are given to churches erected on some particularly memorable occasion, because churches are frequently dedicated to the memory of some event or other out of the life of the Savior or of His Mother, or else of some Saint who is especially honored in some given locality, or whose name was borne by the chief founder of the church.*

When one town or city holds several churches, one of them receives the title of " general " or " universal " (*sobor*), because, on solemn feast days, not only the church's own parishioners, but people from all parishes assemble there for divine service. In large cities there frequently are several general churches. That in which is situated the episcopal *cathedra* or *throne* is called *Cathedral*.

---

*Thus for instance, on the spot where Christ rose from the dead, was built the Church of the Resurrection; in St. Petersburg we have the church named for the Venerable Isaac of Dalmatia, because Peter the Great, the founder of the city, was born on that Saint's day.

Together with the organization on earth of the community of believers in Christ, Christian churches made their appearance, as gathering places for these believers. The Apostles and the early Christians endured persecution for their faith from the heathens, and for that reason used to assemble for prayer in private houses; but even in such houses they used to set apart for worship one room on which they looked with reverence, as on a place where the Lord was present by His grace. When the Christians increased in numbers and room was lacking in private houses for their gatherings, while they were not permitted to build special temples for their own worship, they began to meet together to offer their prayers to God in woods, in mountain gorges and in caves, or, if they lived in cities or in the neighborhood of cities, they assembled in the underground cemeteries known by the name of *Catacombs*. So long as they were persecuted for their faith, they could not decorate the places where they assembled, even though they wished to do so. Still, impelled by their pious feelings, they used, in the place of decorations, certain allegorical signs or *symbols*, intelligible to them alone. Thus, on the walls of the Catacombs, they represented the cross of Christ by the sign **T**; sometimes they drew a square block of stone and on that a door, seeing in this a semblance of Christ, Who is the rock of salvation and the door through which whosoever passeth, shall be saved. Frequently again, Christ was represented in the shape of a fish, because the Greek word for " Fish " *ichthys* is composed of the initials of the words: "*Iesous Christos, Theou Yios, Soter,*" i.e., "*Jesus Christ, Son of God, Savior.*" Still more frequently He is represented as a Lamb, or as a Shepherd, carrying a sheep upon His shoulders. The Resurrection was depicted as the Whale ejecting a man (the Prophet Jonah) out of its maw. At a later time they began to draw the portraits of martyrs somewhere about their tombs in the Catacombs. At that time they performed divine service in garments of the ordinary cut, only they wore their best and most ornamented clothes, preferably white ones. When Christians were allowed to publicly profess their faith, they began to build temples, or rather churches. Sometimes they transformed existing buildings into churches, adapting them to their requirements. But they mostly erected special buildings, which differed from others both in external appearance and internal arrangement. The first churches built by Christians differed from our modern churches in that they had no screen (*ikonostas*), but the sanctuary was separated from the body of the church only by a curtain, or even merely a railing. Besides which, large extensions were added to the ancient churches for the use of catechumens, *i. e.* of persons who had not yet received Holy Baptism, but were preparing to receive it and were undergoing elementary instruction in the Christian faith.

External Appearance of Churches.

The most generally accepted shape for Christian churches is the *oblong, in imitation of a ship*. By giving their churches such a shape, Christians express the thought that, as a ship, under the government of a good helmsman, carries men through stormy seas into a peaceful harbor, so the Church, governed by Christ, saves men from drowning in the deep waters of sin and brings them into the Kingdom of Heaven, "where there is neither sorrow nor sighing." Churches are frequently built in the shape of a *cross*, to show that Christians obtain salvation through faith in Christ crucified, for Whose sake they themselves are ready to suffer all things. Sometimes a church is given the shape of a *circle* in token that the Church of Christ, (*i. e.* the community of those who believe in Christ), shall exist through all eternity and that it will for ever and ever unite the faithful with Christ, for the circle is the emblem of eternity. Sometimes, again, the shape is that of an octagon,—the shape of a *star* in token that, forasmuch as a star shows a man his way on a dark night, so the Church helps him to walk along the path of righteousness amidst the darkness of iniquity which encompasses him. The latter two shapes are not so often used, because inconvenient for the inner arrangement of the church.

The entrance into a church is almost always from the west, the church itself being turned with its main part towards the east, in token that the Christian worshippers enter from the darkness of impiety into the light of truth (the East being the symbol of light, good, truth, while the West is the symbol of darkness, evil, error). This rule is departed from only if a building formerly erected for another purpose is changed into a church, or if a church is arranged in a private house, when the entrance and the main portion are located according to convenience.

On the roof there are usually one or several cupolas (towers with rounded or pointed roofs), signifying that Christians should detach themselves from earthly attachments, and aspire heavenward. These cupolas are called *crests* or *summits*. *One* crest or cupola signifies that the community of Christians has only one head—Christ; *three* cupolas are erected in honor of the Most Holy Trinity; *five* point to Christ and the four Evangelists, who left for us descriptions of Christ's life; while *seven* indicate the Seven Sacraments (through which we receive the seven gifts of the Holy Ghost), and the seven Oecumenic Councils, by the ordinances of which Christians are guided to this day; *nine* crests remind us of the nine classes of angels who dwell in Heaven, whom Christians wish to join in the Kingdom of Heaven, while *thirteen* crests signify Christ and His twelve Apostles. Every cupola, or, where there is none, the roof, is surmounted with a cross, the instrument of our salvation.

The Internal Arrangement of Churches.

The interior of a church is divided into several compartments: 1) the *Sanctuary*, where divine service is performed; 2) the *Chapel of the Prothesis*, containing the *Table of Oblations*, for the reception and preparation of the sacred Gifts; 3) the *Vestry*, for the keeping of sacred objects; 4) the *Body of the Church,* for the worshippers; 5) the *Vestibule* and *Porch,* for the catechumens.

The Sanctuary and Its Belongings.— For those who perform divine service, the eastern part of the church is set aside. It is somewhat raised above the other portion, in order that the service be heard by all present, and is called *the Sanctuary.*

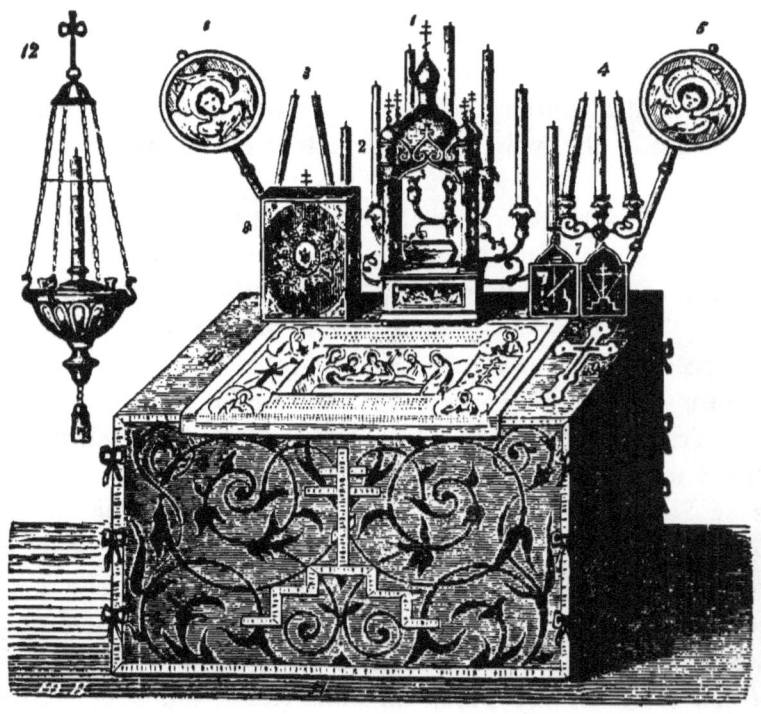

THE ALTAR.

1. The Tabernacle or Ciborium.
2. A Polycandil.
3. The Dykirion.
4. The Trikirion.
5 and 6. The Fans.
7. The Ciborium (to take the Sacrament to the sick).
8. The Testament.
9. The Cross.
10. The Antimins.
11. The Altar Table.
12. A Lampad.

Persons not consecrated to the service of the church are not permitted to enter this part of it. The sanctuary is divided from the worshippers by a curtain, and a partition or screen. In some churches there are several sanctuaries dedicated to the memory of various events and various persons. They are called annexes or chapels.

In the middle of the Sanctuary there stands a square table; it is the altar; also called Holy Throne, because the Lord is present on it, or Holy Table, because upon it Christians are offered the Sacrament of the Eucharist, and made to partake' of the Body and Blood of Christ. The altar is made square, in token that Christ's doctrine and sacrament are free to men of all four parts of the world.

The altar, as being the place on which rests the Glory of the Lord, is vested with two coverings; the first is of white linen, the second or outer covering is of rich brocade. Upon the altar is laid a silken or linen cloth, on which is represented the Descent from the Cross and the preparation of Christ's body for interment. This cloth is called the *Antimins*, which means "what is instead of the altar." The origin of the Antimins is as follows: The law demands that a Christian church shall be consecrated by a bishop; and as there was not always one on hand to do so, and, besides, movable churches had to be organized for travelers, it became usual for bishops to consecrate only the upper boards of the altar, or even only linen or silken cloths, which, after signing them with their name, they sent to new-built churches, or gave to people who were starting on a journey. Later on, an Antimins became a necessary feature of every altar, even in such churches as had been personally consecrated by bishops. Into every Antimins is sewed a particle of some holy relic (i. e. of the incorruptible remains of holy men's bodies) in memory of the fact that in early times Christians used to assemble for divine service on or by the tombs of martyrs, and in token that the Saints, being near to God, intercede for us with their prayers. If the church is consecrated by a bishop, the relic is placed under the center of the altar, upon a stand in a special small casket, to keep it from injury; it is wrapped in a silken cloth called *pleiton*, which means "a wrap."

Indispensable attributes of the altar are the Cross and the Testament*. The Cross is laid there as a sign of Christ's victory over the Devil and of our deliverance, and the Testament, because it is the book which contains the Word of Christ, by following which we may obtain salvation. In the first ages of Christianity, before the execution of criminals by crucifixion had been abolished, Christians used crosses loaded with ornaments, but without the representation of Christ crucified; sometimes only they painted on it a Lamb, either standing at the foot of the Cross or carrying one.

The Testament which is kept on the altar always has a beautiful binding, in the middle of which is a representation of Christ Savior (mostly of the Resurrection), while the corners are occupied by the four Evangelists. These are represented with their respective symbols, in other words, their characteristics, *i. e.* signs which allude to the contents of the books they wrote. With the Apostle Matthew we see the face of a man or an angel, in token that Matthew describes Jesus Christ principally as the Son of Man, the descendant of Abraham, as the Messiah expected by Israel, of whom the prophets wrote. The Evangelist Mark represented Christ as the "Sent of God," possessed of almighty power, the King of all men, whether Jews or Gentiles, and therefore his symbol is the Lion, the mighty king of beasts. The Evangelist Luke, because he represented Christ as the Savior of all mankind, Who offered Himself as a sacrifice for the sins of men, has the Bull, the animal which the Jews used to sacrifice. The Evangelist John has given us more fully than the other Apostles the lofty doctrine of Christ as the Son of God; hence he is associated with the eagle, the bird which soars high and fixes his gaze on the Sun.

---

*We call "Testament," the book which contains the narrative of the earthly life of Christ our Savior, and His teachings. It consists of four books written by the Apostles Matthew, Mark, Luke and John. The Greek work *Evangelion* means "Good News." The description of Christ's earthly life is thus named, because it brings us the good news of our salvation. Hence the Apostles, who have written the Savior's Life, are named "evangelists," which means "bringers of good news."

Besides the Cross and Testament there stands on the altar an ark or tabernacle, in which are preserved the Holy Gifts (the Body of Christ, saturated with His Blood), reserved for giving communion to the sick, and to others at times when it is not lawful to celebrate the Liturgy. These tabernacles are sometimes made in the shape of a coffin, or a sepulchral cave, in which case they are called " Graves;"—at other times in the shape of a temple. A temple-shaped tabernacle, used, in old times, to be called " Zion " or " Jerusalem."* All tabernacles alike are called " Ciboriums." The ciborium used to carry the Holy Gifts into a private house, in order to give communion to a sick person, is a casket with several compartments. In one is placed a very small casket containing particles of the Holy Gifts. In another there is a small chalice with a tiny spoon, and in a third a small vessel with wine and a sponge to clean the chalice with. Ciboriums also are kept on the altar.

The space behind the altar is called *Bema* or " high place," because it is sometimes raised above the rest of the Sanctuary. On this spot is placed the *Cathedra* or throne of the Bishop, and on both sides of it are seats for the priests. In our day the episcopal Cathedrae are placed only in the principal (general) churches (*Sobor*), which hence are called Cathedrals. On the eastern side of the church above the Bema, is a representation of the Savior, and on both sides of it, are ikons of Apostles, but more often of holy bishops. The lampad before the ikon of the Bema is called *High Light*. In very ancient churches where the eastern wall always had a window, the Sacrament of the Eucharist was represented on both sides of it: on one side Christ giving to six apostles His Body under the form of bread, and on the other side Christ giving communion to the other six apostles out of the cup filled with His Blood under the form of wine.

* Jerusalem was the ancient capital of the Hebrews; Zion was a mountain near Jerusalem on which were built the palaces of David and Solomon. Christians began to give these names to the kingdom of Heaven, which they hoped to reach through Christ, who suffered for the sins of men near the earthly Jerusalem, and later on to the tabernacles in which the Holy Gifts are kept through part aking of which in communion they hoped to receive salvation.

Sometimes a canopy is erected over the altar, on four columns, and beneath it hovers a dove with outspread wings, a symbol of the Holy Ghost.

The Chapel of the Prothesis and its belongings.—On the left-hand side of the Sanctuary is placed the chapel of the *Prothesis* or "offering." That is where the offerings of Christians towards divine service are received. This chapel sometimes forms a separate compartment, divided from the sanctuary by a wall

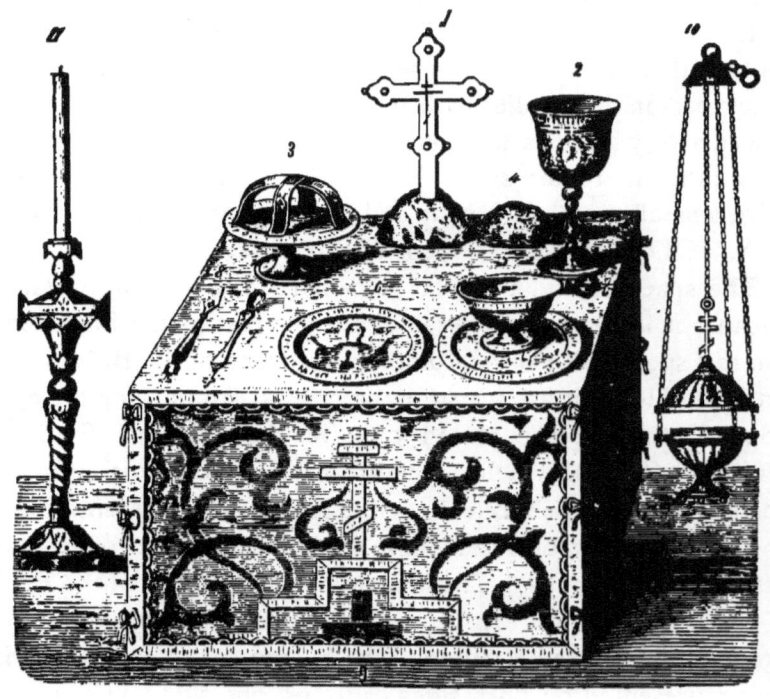

THE TABLE OF OBLATIONS.

1. The Cross.
2. The Chalice.
3. The Paten and Asterisk.
5. The Dipper.
6. The Dishes.
7. The Spoon.
8. The Lance.
9. The Table.
10. The Censer.
11. A Candlestick with Candle.

with a door, or only by columns or a curtain. In most churches, however, it is connected with the Sanctuary. In this space there always is a table whereon are deposited the offerings. It is called the *Table of Oblations* and vested with rich coverings, like the altar; the wall around it is decorated with ikons. On this table are also placed the sacred vessels used in the preparation of the Sacrament of the Eucharist. They are the following:

The *Paten* or *Disk* (which means a round dish) on which are laid the portions of bread cut out in memory of Christ, the Mother of God and the Saints; also for the good of the living and the dead. For greater convenience the paten is now made with a foot. To it belong two small dishes or plates. On one of these plates is laid the bread, out of which a portion has been taken in memory of Christ; the top of it is stamped in the middle with a cross, while around the rim runs the inscription: "Thy Cross we worship, O Lord." On the other plate is laid the bread from which a portion has been taken out in honor of the Mother of God; it is stamped with an effigy of her and the inscription around the rim reads as follows: "Meet it is to honor Thee as being in truth the Mother of God."

The *Asterisk*, consisting of two arched bands, held by a screw in such a way, that they may be put together, or turned around into the shape of a cross. It is placed over the paten, to prevent the portions of bread, which are laid on it in a certain order from getting mixed up.

The *Lance*.—A lance-shaped knife, double-edged, used to take portions out of the bread.

The *Chalice* or *Poterion* ("a drinking cup"), into which is poured wine mixed with water during the preparation of the Sacrament. To it belongs a small dipper, in which wine and water is presented.

The *Spoon*, with which the Holy Sacrament,—the Body and Blood of Christ,—is administered to communicants.

The *Sponge*, which is used for cleaning the holy vessels after the Liturgy. In our church two sponges are used. With one the paten is wiped, after the portions of bread have been dropped into the chalice; this sponge is kept on the altar in the Antimins and called "Antimins sponge." The other, which is used to wipe the chalice after it has been washed, is kept on the Table of Oblations, and is called the "cleansing sponge."

The Veils—one of which covers the paten, another the chalice, and a third both paten and chalice together—are used to protect the Holy Gifts against dust and insects. These veils are also called *Aërs*, because they cover the holy vessels even as air covers the earth; the largest veil is especially known under this name.

The Fans are used for driving insects from the Holy Gifts, when the veils are removed. In ancient times they used to be made of peacocks' feathers, linen or fine leather. At the present time they are made of metal, in the form of a circle, somewhat like the glory around a saint's head, and with a long handle; in the middle of the circle a cherub is represented. These fans are used only at pontifical services, and are to remind us that cherubs worship God with us before His altar.

The Vestry and its belongings.— On the right hand of the Sanctuary a space is partitioned off and called vestry. Here are preserved the church vessels, the books which are used in the performance of the services, and the vestments of those who officiate in them. As all these articles are in charge of the deacons, the vestry is also called *diakonnikon*. In ancient times all sorts of edible gifts for the clerics used to be brought there, such as boiled rice or wheat (*kutyá*), cheese, eggs, sweet Easter cheese (*pasclta*).

The Nave or Body of the Church.—The Sanctuary, together with the Prothesis and vestry, are divided from the space provided for the worshippers by a grating or screen, which is called the *Ikonostas* ("image stand"), because it is decorated with ikons or sacred images. The Ikonostas has three doors. The folding doors in the middle, which lead into the Sanctuary, to the altar, are called the Holy Gates, because the Holy Gifts of the Eucharist are brought out through them, or the Royal Gates, because the King of Glory, Jesus Christ, passes through them in the Holy Eucharist. These doors are generally in open-work and decorated with carving and ikons. These latter usually represent the Annunciation and the four Evangelists, with their symbols or characteristics, to signify that on the altar is offered the sacrifice for the salvation of mankind, the first tidings of which were received by the Virgin Mary from the Archangel Gabriel, as known to us from the narratives of the four Evangelists. Just behind the Royal Gates a curtain is hung. During the services the Royal Gates are opened for the celebrants to go in and out of the Sanctuary, while the curtain is drawn across or drawn away, even when the Royal Gates are closed, in order to emphasize certain prayers or the meaning of certain rites. Thus during penitential services, such as Complines, Midnight Vigils and the Canonical Hours, the curtain remains drawn, in token that our sins remove us far away from heaven, from God. During solemn, joyous services, assuring us that the Lord hath saved us, such as Vespers and Matins, it is drawn away. During the Liturgy, the curtain remains drawn away almost all the time. The door on the left of the Royal Gates leads into the Prothesis and is called the "northern door," while that on the right leads into the vestry and is called the "southern" or "deacons' door." On these two doors there are usually paintings representing either angels—the messengers of God, who minister unto Him in the Kingdom of Heaven —or sainted deacons, who in their lifetime, had charge of the Prothesis and vestry.

Besides the decorations of the doors, the entire screen which separates the sanctuary from the nave is decorated with ikons, in one, two, or more tiers. Such screens, therefore, differ in appearance: they are either like an open-work grating, varying in height, or a solid wall up to the ceiling. The ikons of the first tier are called "local ikons." On the right of the Royal Gates there is always an ikon of the Savior, and next to it the "church ikon," *i. e.* a representation of the Saint or event, in honor of whom or which the church has been named and dedicated. On the left side is an ikon of the Mother of God. In the same tier, if there is room, are usually placed the ikons of such Saints as are most honored in a given locality. Above the Royal Gates it is usual to place a painting of the Last Supper, in token that, in partaking of Christ's Holy Sacrament, men are made worthy of entering into the Kingdom of Heaven. The second tier is the place for the presentation of the different church feasts, *i. e.* of the principal events in the lives of our Lord and His Mother. The third tier contains the ikons of the Apostles and in the middle of them, just above that of the Last Supper, is a representation of Jesus Christ—the subject of their preaching—in royal or episcopal vestments, with His Mother at His right hand and the Precursor at the left. Such a presentation of Christ, bears the special name of *Deisus*.* If there is a fourth tier, it is filled with the ikons of Old Testament prophets and in the middle of them is the Mother of God with the Divine Infant. A fifth and sixth tier will hold ikons of holy martyrs and sainted bishops. The very top of the Ikonostas is adorned with the cross, bearing the effigy of Jesus crucified. An Ikonostas decorated in this manner, brings before us all the denizens of heaven and serves as a book, from which even those who cannot read may learn the history of Christ's church and her doctrine.

The Ikonostas does not stand on the very edge of the raised floor of the sanctuary, but so that part of this floor projects into the nave. The part of the platform in front of the screen is called the *Soleas* (which means " an elevated place "). On this elevation Christians stand to receive Holy Communion, and the celebrants come out of the sanctuary and stand there while they recite public prayers and speak instructive addresses or read portions of Scripture. On both sides are placed the readers and singers. The middle of the platform just in front of the Royal Gates, where Holy Communion is administered, prayers and addresses are read, is called the *Ambo*, which means *Ascent*, and the place set apart at each end for the readers and singers is called *Cleros*. The word means *lots*. These places are called

---

*Christ is represented in royal garments, because He is the King Who founded the Kingdom of God on earth, and in episcopal vestments because He is the High-Priest Who offered Himself in sacrifice for the sins of man. The name of *Deisus* given to such an ikon is derived by some from the Greek word *Deisis*, which means " prayer." It is probable that in ancient times a prayer was written below the ikon, probably with the heading: " *Deisis* " and men ignorant of the Greek tongue, took the word for the name of the ikon.

thus because in early times the readers and singers were chosen by lots.

Near each Cleros are kept the portable ikons, *i. e.* those which are used for divine services outside the church. They are fastened to long handles, sometimes by loops, more frequently by cords, and have the shape of banners. Indeed they are called banners, for they represent the banners of the church, under which Christians, being the warriors of Christ's kingdom, go forth to fight the foes of truth and love.

1. The Ikonostas.
2. The Royal Gates.
3. The Northern and Southern Doors.
4. The Soleas.
5. The Ambo.
6. The Cleros.
7. The Banners.

The space in front of the Soleas is reserved for the worshippers; the walls, as well as the square pillars which support the cupolas, are decorated with ikons and paintings representing events from the history of Christ's church.

Over against the Royal Gates, on the western side of the church, is an entrance door leading into the vestibule, and called the "beautiful door," because it usually is richly decorated,— also simply the "church door," because leading into the church.

In large churches there are other smaller doors in the northern and southern sides of the church; through these the worshippers can go out into the side vestibules and to the porches.

Vestibule and Porch.— The vestibule is divided into two parts, the inner and the outer, the latter being called porch. The inner porch, used, in the early ages, to be set apart for catechumens,—persons who wished to become Christians, were receiving Christian instruction and preparing for baptism,—and for penitents, *i. e.* for Christians who, for their sins, were refused communion. In the vestibule was placed the fount for the performance of baptism; here, also, Christians used to take their food at a common table after the end of divine service. In monasteries the vestibule to this day serves as dining-room or refectory. It is in the vestibules that the church orders the penitential services to be performed, in order more clearly to show that men remove themselves farther away from God by their sins and become unworthy to stand within His temple. In the outer vestibule or porch the "weepers" used to stand in ancient times,—a class of penitents who were forbidden to enter the church, and here implored the prayers of those who went in. In the East funeral services over the bodies of departed Christians are held on the porch.

At the present time the number of grown up catechumens is not large; public excommunications almost never occur, and common meals after divine service have also fallen into disuse: there is therefore no need of spacious vestibules. In some churches there still are small vestibules; but in most of them there are no inner vestibules at all, but only porches, which have become the gathering place of beggars.

Appurtenances of Public Divine Service in Churches.

Illumination: Lampads, Candelabra and Candlesticks.—In all churches, on the altar and on the Table of Oblations, also behind the altar and in front of the ikons, lights are kept burning, not only during evening and night services, but during day services as well. They signify that the Lord gives us the light of truth, and that our souls burn with the love of God and are penetrated with feelings of joy and devotion. It is quite in accordance with this conception, that the illumination of the church is increased during solemn holiday services and decreased during penitential services.

For the illumination of a church, two things are needed—oil and wax. Oil (yielded by the fruit of the olive tree), is symbolic of grace, indicating that the Lord sheds His grace on men, while men on their side are ready to offer Him in sacrifice deeds of mercy. The pure wax, collected by the bees from fragrant flowers, is used as a token that the prayers of men offered from a pure heart are acceptable to God.

Of the candlesticks and candelabra used in the church, some are portable and some stationary, all varying in the number of candles or lamps which they bear. The candlesticks are always portable and carry one, two or three candles. One candle reminds us that there is but one God, Who is the Light Eternal; the candlestick with two candles is called *Dykirion* ("two candles"), and indicates that in Jesus Christ are united two natures—the divine and the human; that of three candles is called *Trikirion* ("three candles"), and alludes to the three persons of the Deity. There are stationary candelabra, standing or suspended, in front of the ikons, bearing both oil lamps and wax candles. These are called *candils* or *lampads* if they carry only one candle; *polycandils* ("many lights"), if they carry seven or twelve candles (seven candles in allusion to the seven gifts of the Holy Ghost, and twelve in allusion to the Apostles); lastly *panicandils* ("all light") are those that carry more than twelve candles. Sometimes, if a panicandil is made in the shape of a circle, garnished with candles, it is called *khoros*, which means "a circle," "an assembly."

Incense.—Besides the lampads, candlesticks and candelabra, with their burning candles and lamps, an important item of divine service is the burning and swinging of incense (a fragrant tree-gum). This swinging is performed sometimes before the altar and the ikons; then it expresses the wish of the worshippers that their prayer may ascend to Heaven, as the fumes of the incense mount aloft. Sometimes the incense is swung towards the worshippers; then it expresses the wish of the celebrant that the grace of the Holy Ghost may encompass these souls of the faithful as the fragrant cloud of the incense encompasses them. The vessel which holds the incense is called *censer;* it is a cup with a cover running on three slight chains, which all unite into one handle.

Bellringing.—Every church has bells. They are placed either on the roof, in the turrets of the cupolas, or at the entrance above the porch, in the so-called " bell-chamber," or else next to the church in specially erected structures called " belfries." If the bell-chamber is made in the shape of a tall turret above the porch, it is also usually called a belfry.

The bells are used to call the faithful to divine service,—to express the triumph of the Church,—and to announce the principal acts of the service to those Christians who are not present at it, in order that they may join mentally in the common prayers of the worshippers. There are three ways of ringing the bells, according to the object for which they are rung:

1) One bell is struck several times at short intervals. That is done before the beginning of the service, to announce that it is about to begin, and is called *the toll.* In the same way is announced the moment of the Liturgy when the Great Mystery is accomplished, and sometimes the reading of the Gospel in other services. Where there are many bells, different ones are used on different days, and then they have different names—such as the " feast bell," the " Sunday bell," the " week-day bell," the " small bell."

2) Several bells are struck together three different times, in a "*peal.*" This is usually done at the beginning of solemn services (the Liturgy, Vespers and Matins), after the single-stroke toll. On high feast-days the bells are rung in this way all day.

3) Every bell is struck once in turn, and after having gone over all the bells in this way two or three times, they are struck all together. This is called a *carillon*, and is reserved for special occasions, such as the bringing out of the Cross and the Sepulchre on Good Fridays and during processions.

OF THE PERSONS WHO PERFORM DIVINE SERVICE AND OF THEIR VESTMENTS.

The Clergy.

The persons who take part in the performance of divine services are divided into *celebrants* and *church servitors*. Only those persons are called celebrants who have received the grace of the Holy Ghost, through the Sacrament of Orders; they are the Bishops, the Priests and the Deacons.

The first and highest degree of priesthood belongs to the Bishop (*Episcopos*, which means "overseer"). This name is given to the successors of the Apostles in the service and government of the Church; with regard to public divine service, bishops are the chiefs or heads of all the churches situated in their diocese. They dedicate churches, consecrate Antiminses, give authority for the performance of services in these churches, and appoint all those who hold any office in them. During services the bishops, as the highest performers of all Sacraments through which the grace of the Holy Ghost is imparted to men, bless Christians with both hands, and, in their capacity of chief teachers and enlighteners of the faithful, they also bless them with lighted candles—the *Dykirion* and *Trikirion*. When giving the blessing they compose the fingers of the right hand in such a manner as to form the name of Jesus Christ in Greek. To accomplish this, the index is stretched out straight and the middle finger slightly bent, thus representing the letters "IC;" then the annular is bent, the thumb is laid across it, and the little finger is slightly inclined, forming the letters "XC." This way of composing the fingers is called *nominal*. In his capacity of chiefs over the priests, otherwise called *hierei*, a bishop also has the title of *Arch-hiereus*. All bishops are equal among themselves, owing to their common grace of priesthood. But as the districts subject to their jurisdiction differ in size and importance, as regarded in earthly kingdoms and empires, there are grades in the titles of bishops: those who have charge only of small districts or cities are called simply Bishops or *Arch-hierei;* those whose jurisdiction extends over larger cities and provinces have lately begun to assume the title of "Arch-bishop" (*i.e.* chief, first among the bishops); the bishop of a capital city, otherwise called "metropolis," is entitled "Metropolitan"; the bishops of ancient capitals of the great Roman Empire (Rome, Constantinople, Antioch) and of Jerusalem—the cities from which the Christian faith spread over the globe,—have received the title of "Patriarch" (which means "chief over the fathers"). A bishop sometimes has an assistant, who is also a bishop; these subordinate bishops are called "Vicars," *i. e* "lieutenants." In some countries, as for instance, in our own, the churches are governed by an assembly of several bishops; such an assembly is known by the name of "Synod."

The second degree of ordained priesthood is occupied by the *hierei* or Priests, who, by the authority and blessing of their bishops, govern small Christian communities, called "parishes," and have in their charge the parish churches. They bless the beginning of every public divine service, perform all the sacraments of the church with the exception of ordination, and have under their supervision all the persons who hold any office in these churches. They also have the right to give their blessing in the name of the Lord to those inferior to them in spiritual rank, but only with one hand. All priests are equal as regards the grace of priesthood; but there are differences among them, according to the importance of the churches and parishes committed to their care. Some are called simply priests or *hierei*, others receive the title of "arch-priests" or *proto-hierei*, (i. e. "first" or "senior priest"); arch-priests have the precedence when they perform services together with priests of the lower rank. The priests of churches attached to imperial palaces, to a Patriarchate and the Synod have the title of *presbyter* ("elder") and the chief priest of such a church takes that of *proto-presbyter.* Priests who have taken monastic vows are called *hiero-monachi,* which means " priest-monks."

The Deacon holds the third degree of priesthood. Deacon means " ministrant." He ministers to the bishop and to the priests in the performance of the sacraments, but may not perform them himself, and therefore has not the right to bless in the name of the Lord. At public divine service he, by the priest's blessing, recites the common prayers, reads portions from the Holy Scriptures, and sees that the worshippers comport themselves decorously. In the degree of their ordination all deacons are equal; yet there are different grades among them. The senior deacons of the principal churches are called *proto-deacons* and claim precedence when they officiate with other deacons; and the chief deacon attached to the person of a bishop receives the title of arch-deacon. If a deacon is also a monk he is called *hiero-deacon.*

Church Servitors (clerics and acolytes) are persons appointed to certain services in a church used as a place of worship. The highest position among these is that of the " sub-deacons " or *hypo-deacons;* they assist at pontifical services and therefore are found only in Cathedral churches. After them come the Readers and choristers, also called " clerks " and " psalm-readers," and the sacristans or doorkeepers (janitors). Part of the latter's duty is to keep the church neat and clean and to ring the bells. During service they bring out the candlesticks and the censer, and when they have done with these duties, they take part in the reading and singing. All the church servitors together make up the " church staff," because they are attached to the church. They are also called " clerics " or, collectively, the " kleros," because in ancient times they used to be appointed by lot. Sometimes the celebrants are included in the kleros, which then might better be called the " clergy," and is divided into " higher " and " lower." The higher clergy includes the celebrants—bishops, priests and deacons; the lower includes the church servitors.

The Sacred Vestments.

The Antiquity of the Vestments.— In the very earliest times of Christianity, persons officiating in a church used to wear, while performing divine service, the same kind of garments as those worn by laymen. But a feeling of reverence prompted them to appear at the common worship in clean, festive garments. The favorite color for such occasions was white, in token that church service demands holiness and purity. The garments for the celebrants were provided by the community; they were kept in secret places and given out to the celebrants when they prepared for the services. Such is the origin of church vestments or holy garments. In the course of time the cut of laymen's garments changed; various peoples adopted new fashions; only the cut of church vestments, used while officiating in divine services, remained unaltered and universally the same, in token of the unity and immutable nature of the faith and as an allusion to the qualities demanded of the ministers of the Church. All these garments were, from the earliest times, decorated with crosses, to distinguish them from ordinary garments.

The Sticharion or Tunic.—The universal garment worn by all ancient nations, men and women alike, was the *Chiton*, otherwise called *Tunic* or *Sticharion*, a long garment with sleeves, which reached to the ground. This garment remains common to all classes of ordained persons, with this small difference, that the deacon's tunic has wide sleeves, while the priest's and bishop's tunics have tight-fitting ones. By its brilliant whiteness this garment reminds the celebrant that the grace of the Holy Ghost covers him as with a garment of salvation and joy; and invests him with beauty. In our days, the members of the lower clergy are also authorized to wear this garment.

The Orarion and the Epitrachelion.—Another indispensable portion of every man's dress was the towel or scarf, which every one wore, thrown over one shoulder and sometimes both. Poor people used it to wipe their mouth and face after ablutions; while wealthy men of rank, who had slaves to carry their towel for them, used the scarf which they wore themselves as an ornament, and therefore had it made out of rich stuffs and sometimes decorated with pearls and precious stones. Such a scarf was called an *Orarion*. The *Orarion*—or *Stole*—remained as one of the sacred vestments, to be used by all classes of ordained persons, in token that the grace of the Holy Ghost flows down upon them abundantly. Deacons wear it on the left shoulder and only on certain occasions bind it around their bodies crosswise. The Orarion is the deacon's principal vestment, without which he cannot officiate at any service whatever. Holding one end of it with his right hand, he slightly raises it, when he invites the congregation to begin prayers and to listen attentively; also when he himself recites prayers. In old times, deacons used to wipe the lips of communicants with the Orarion after they had received the Eucharist. Because deacons minister on earth around the Lord's altar as the angels surround Him in the heavens, so, in allusion thereto, the angelic hymn: " Holy, holy, holy, the Lord Sabaoth!" formerly used to be embroidered on the Orarion. Priests and bishops wear this garment on both shoulders, in such a manner that it encircles their neck and descends in front in two ends, which, for convenience sake, are either sewed or buttoned together. From this way of wearing it, the priest's Orarion or double stole has the name of *Epitrachelion*, which means "what is worn around the neck." Priests and bishops thus wear the Orarion on both shoulders in token that they have received the added grace of priesthood and have devoted themselves wholly to the Church. Of the church servitors only the sub-deacons wear the Orarion, crossed on the shoulders or tied under one shoulder.

The Maniples and Zone, or Belt.—To the ancient costume also belonged the *Maniples*—a sort of cuffs, under which men used to gather at the wrist the wide sleeves of the *chiton* or tunic,—and the *Zone* or *belt*, which they girded round their waists, when they prepared for any work or went on travels. Maniples still remain an attribute of all grades of priesthood, as an indication that a minister of the Church must hope, not in his own strength, but in the help of God. The belt is worn only by priests or bishops, and serves to remind them that God strengthens them with His own strength, places them on the path of

THE SACRED VESTMENTS.

1. The Sticharion.
2. The Orarion.
3. The Phelonion.
4. The Epitrachelion.
5. The Maniples.
6. The Zone.
7. The Thigh-shield.
8. The Epigonation.
9. The Scuffia.
10. The Kamilavka.
11. The Mitre.
12. The Saccos and the Omophorion.
13. The Pectoral Cross.
14. The Panagia.
15. The Orlets rug.
16. The Crozier.

righteousness, and helps them to ascend to the height of holiness with the fleetness of the deer.

The Phelonion or Cope and the Saccos.—Over the
chiton or tunic the ancients used to wear a garment named *Phelonion*. It was long, wide, sleeveless, enveloping the entire person, and leaving only one opening for the head. Poor people made it out of some thick, coarse stuff, and used it only in traveling, to protect them from cold and bad weather. The rich wore the same garment, made out of soft material, so that it was not only a protection in traveling, but an ornamental cloak. It was contrived so as to enable the wearer to get out and use his hands. To this effect there were studs on the shoulders, over which were looped cords which, being pulled, shirred up the skirt of the garment. When shirred up on both shoulders to leave both hands free, it presented the aspect of two bags, one of which—the larger—hung down behind, and the other, smaller, in front. The Phelonion has been preserved as one of the priestly vestments, in token that priests are invested with truth, and hedged off by it from all the iniquities which surround them, and consequently should be ministers of the truth. In Eastern churches the Phelonion is still made after the old model, of equal length in front and behind. But in Russian churches, where this vestment is made out of the richest cloths, of gold and silver, which it would be difficult to shirr up on the shoulders, it is cut out in front, so that it is much shorter than behind. The Phelonion is usually called simply " robe " (*reeza*).

For several centuries the Phelonion was worn also by bishops. But, when the Christian faith became predominant, the Greek Emperors granted to the principal bishops—the Patriarchs,—the right of wearing the *Dalmatic*,—a garment like a short tunic with short sleeves, or half sleeves,—worn only by themselves and the grandees of the Empire. The bishops adopted this garment, not as a worldly adornment, but as a reminder that they must rise to holiness of life, and called it *Saccos*, which means a " sackcloth garment," or " garment of humility." In the course of time it became common to all bishops, and they wear it now in the place of the Phelonion.

The Omophorion.—In ancient times aged men and persons in poor health used to wear on their shoulders, over the Phelonion, to keep themselves warm, a sheepskin, which was called *Omophorion,* i. e. " shoulder covering." Some bishops, especially the more aged, wore the sheepskin even during divine service, laying it aside at the most solemn moments. Soon the Omophorion was added to the church vestments, as one distinctively belonging to bishops. It was made at first out of sheepskin, afterwards out of white woolen stuff; but now it is of the same material as the rest of the vestments. It is a long broad strip, adorned with crosses and arranged on the bishop's shoulders in such a way that one end descends in front and the other behind. This vestment reminds the bishop, that he should take thought for the conversion of the erring, as a merciful shepherd, who takes the straying sheep upon his shoulders.

The Mitre, the Skull-cap ("Kamilavka") and the Scuffia.—The headdress of the ancients was a long strip of linen cloth, which was wrapped around the head and called " head-band " or " fillet." According to the position and wealth of the wearer, this head-gear differed in material and shape. At first only Patriarchs adopted it during divine service; but in the course of time it became a part of the sacred vestments of all bishops. At the present time archimandrites, archpriests and some priests are given the right to wear a head-dress during divine service. That of the bishops is called a *mitre* (which means " headband "); the head-dresses of priests are called, one kind—the skull-cap—*kamilavka,* and the other, *scuffia.* The word *kamilavka* means either " something made out of camel's hair," or " somethings that protects against heat;" while *scuffia* means " something resembling a cup or a skull."

The Epigonation or " Pálitsa," and the Thigh-shield (" Nabédrennik").—In ancient times persons occupying important positions in the armies and at courts wore swords of different kinds, and under them, suspended from the belt, knee-protectors, also varying in form. They were either oblong squares, tied to the belt by two cords or strings, or smaller and lozenge-shaped pieces, tied by one string. The knee-protectors of the first kind were called "thigh-shields" (in Russian *nabédrennik*); those of the second—*epigonation* (in Russian *pálitsa*). These articles, as well as the weapons which rested on them, were signs of distinction conferred on State servants. The Greek Emperors, after they became Christians, granted to the bishops and a few priests the right of wearing them without swords; thus they were added to the church vestments as *signs of distinction*. Those who receive the right of wearing the thigh-shield alone, suspend it on the right side; if the *epigonation* is added, the latter is worn on the right side and the thigh-shield on the left. The priests and bishops to whom these signs of distinction are granted, wear them as a reminder that they have received the spiritual sword—the Word of God, with which they must smite all that is impure and vicious.

To recapitulate: The *tunic* or *sticharion* is the garment of the reader; that of the sub-deacon is the tunic with the *orarion* or stole, always folded round the person; deacons have the tunic, the stole and the *maniples*, priests—the tunic, the *epitrachelion* or double stole, the maniples, the *belt,* and the *phelonion* or outer robe; and some have, in addition to these, the *thigh-shield*, the *epigonation*, the *kamilavka* or skull-cap, and the *scuffia*. The vestments of a bishop are: The *tunic*, the *epitrachelion*, the *belt*, the *maniples*, the *thigh-shield*, the *epigonation*, the *saccos*, the *omophorion* and the *mitre*.

The Pectoral Cross, the Panagia, the Crozier and the Orlets ("Eaglet").—These form part of the special attributions and adornments of bishops at the present day.

They wear a cross on their breast, outside their robes, as a reminder that they should not merely carry Christ in their hearts, but also confess him in the face of all men, *i. e.* that they must be preachers of the faith of Christ. Such crosses, ornamented in various ways, are given as signs of distinction to all the archimandrites, also and to several archpriests and priests.

The *Panagia* ("which means the All-holy") is a round or oval image of the Savior or the Mother of God, not large, but richly decorated, which bishops wear on the breast. It is also given to some archimandrites. In old times *panagias* were made of somewhat different shape—that of a folding dyptich, round or square, on one side of which was the image of the Virgin, on the other that of the Savior or of the Holy Trinity. There also was a receptacle for holding particles of holy relics.

The *Crozier* or pastoral staff is nowadays used by all bishops in token that they are shepherds of Jesus' flock and should care for it as a father for his children. For this reason the crozier is also called *paterissa* (from the Greek word *pater*—" father "). The episcopal crozier has a double crook on top and above that—a cross. The crook is usually made like serpents' heads at both ends, in memory of the Savior's words: " Be wise like unto serpents." As the serpent is renovated yearly, casting off its old slough and forcing its way through thorny plants, so the bishop, while guiding his flock, must follow himself and lead others along the path of enlightenment and renovation, in despite of sorrows and sufferings. Below the crook, a piece of some kind of handsome cloth is tied, usually silk, as an ornament, and to make it pleasanter to the hand to hold the staff.

The *Orlets* (" Eaglet ") is a small round or oval rug, whereon is represented an eagle, with a glory around his head, flying above a city. During divine service, the bishop stands on such rugs, as a reminder that he should, by his teaching and his life, rise above his flock, and be to them the example of a soul aspiring from the things of earth to those of heaven.

ON PUBLIC WORSHIP.

The Daily, Weekly, and Yearly Cycles of Services.

Public worship consists of various collections of prayers, or church services. All these services are adapted to the twenty-four hours of the day. They express our remembrance of events which happened at certain hours, and contain petitions suited to these memories.

The Daily Cycle of Services.—In ancient times days were counted from the evening. At six o'clock p. m. (as *we* count time), *night* began, which was divided into the following four portions or *watches* (times of changing sentries): *evening* (from 6 to 9 p. m. as we would say); *midnight* (from 9 p. m. to 12); the *cock-crow* (from 12 to 3 a. m.), and *morning* (from 3 to 6 a. m.). The day began at 6 a. m. by our reckoning, and was also divided into four watches or *hours*: The *first* hour or *Prime* (6 to 9 a. m.); the *third* hour or *Terce* (from 9 a. m. to 12 or noon); the *sixth* hour or *Sext* (from 12 to 3 p. m.), and the *ninth* hour or *None* (from 3 to 6 p. m.). Christians begin each portion of the day by common prayer. This resulted in eight services: *Vespers, Complines, Nocturns* and *Matins* for the night; the services of the First, Third, Sixth, Ninth Hours for the day. Besides these, in fulfillment of Christ's command to break bread in memory of him, Christians celebrate every day the Liturgy, or, if not the liturgy—the *Typica*, otherwise called the "Pro-Liturgy Service." Thus was formed a daily cycle of nine services.

The Weekly Cycle of Services.—Every day of the *sennight* or *week* is consecrated to certain special memories, as follows: *Sunday*, to that of Christ's rising from the dead; *Monday*, to honoring the holy Angels; *Tuesday*, to the memory of the Prophets and, among them, of the greatest among prophets, John the Precursor; *Wednesday*, is consecrated to the Cross of Christ, as being the day of Judas' treason; *Thursday*, to the memory of all sainted bishops and, in the number, of Nicholas, Bishop of Myra in Lycia; *Friday*, to the Cross, as being the day of the Crucifixion; *Saturday*, to the Saints, especially to the Mother of God, and to the memory of all those who have died in the hope of resurrection and eternal life. The remembrance of these events and persons is recalled by certain prayers and anthems, different for each day of the week, which enter into the fixed daily cycle of services. Besides which, the services for Saturday and especially those for Sunday, are celebrated with greater solemnity, as being feast-day services; while the services of Wednesday and Friday are consecrated to penance, and are accompanied by severe fast all through the year, with the exception of six weeks in the year, when the fasts are suspended in honor of special memories. These weeks are called *unbroken* weeks, because not broken by fasts. They are the two weeks after Christmas day, the week of the Publican and the Pharisee, the week before the beginning of Lent, the Easter week and the week preceding the Pentecost. Such are the peculiar features of every day of the week, and thus is formed *the weekly cycle of services.*

The Yearly Cycle.—Every day of every month, every day of the year is consecrated to the memory of certain events or to that of different Saints. In honor of each given event or person, special anthems, prayers and rites have been established, which are added to the anthems and prayers for the day of the week, introducing more new features into the fixed routine of the daily services—features which change with every day of the year. This forms *the yearly cycle of services.*

Feasts.—In the yearly cycle, the greatest changes in the service occur on great feast-days and during the fasts. According to the subjects of the services, the feast-days are divided into *Feasts of Our Lord,* in honor of God Himself,—*of the Mother of God,*—and *Saints' Feasts,* in honor of the holy angels and of holy men. According to the solemnity of the services, they are divided into *great, medium,* and *lesser*; according to the time of celebration, into *fixed,* i. e. such as return periodically on the same dates of the same month in each year,—and *movable, i. e.* such as occur yearly on the same days of the week, but on different dates and even in different months, following the movements of the Paschal Feast.

The Paschal Feast.—(Easter Sunday), as being the day of the Resurrection of Our Lord, is the feast of feasts. Besides this feast there are twelve more, some fixed, some movable, which are distinguished by services of especial solemnity. They are called the *Twelve Feasts.* Of these some are established in honor of the Lord, others of the Mother of God. The former are: The *Nativity of Christ* (Christmas), 25th of December,—the *Epiphany* (Twelfth Night) 6th of January;—the *Transfiguration*, 6th of August;—the *Entrance into Jerusalem* (Palm Sunday), the Sunday before Easter;—the *Ascension*, on the fortieth day after Easter;—*Pentecost*, in commemoration of the Descent of the Holy Ghost on the Apostles, on the fiftieth day after Easter,—and the Day of the *Exaltation of the Holy Cross*, in memory of the finding and setting up ("exalting") for public adoration of the Cross on which Christ was crucified, 14th of September. The feasts celebrated in honor of the Virgin are: Her *Nativity*, 8th of September;—her *Presentation in the Temple*, 21st of November;—the *Annunciation*, 25th of March;—the *Presentation in the Temple of the Infant Jesus* (Candlemas), 2d of February,—and the *Decease of the Mother of God* (Assumption), 15th of August.* There are days preceding and following each of the twelve feasts, during which the anthems belonging to the feast are sung at all services. Over and above this, the day following upon many of the Twelve Feasts is consecrated to the memory of the persons who took part in the event which the feast commemorates. Thus the day after that of the Nativity of Christ is called " the Congress of the Virgin," *i. e.* the congregation meets to do honor to the Mother of God; the day after the Epiphany there is a service in honor of St. John the Baptist; the day after the Pentecost,—in honor of the Holy Ghost; the day after the Nativity of the Virgin—in honor of her parents St. Joachim and St. Anna; the day after the Annunciation is called " the Congress of the Archangel Gabriel;" the day after the Presentation of the Infant Jesus— " the Congress of the holy Simeon and Anna the Prophetess." The Church prepares for some of the feasts by fasts and special prayers for the dead.

The substance of the anthems for the various festivals is contained in the *Troparion*—or verse—for the day. *Troparion for the day of the Nativity of the Virgin:* " Thy Nativity, O Virgin, Mother of of God, hath brought gladness to the whole universe; for from thee

---

*The events in commemoration of which these feasts were established, are known from Sacred History; therefore they are not related here. The entire narrative of the finding of the Holy Cross belongs to the History of the Church.

hath risen the Sun of Righteousness, Christ our God; yea, having loosed the curse, He hath given a blessing; and having brought to naught death, hath granted us life eternal."—*Troparion for the day of the Presentation of the Virgin:* "To-day is the fore-shadowing of the goodwill of God, and the pre-heralding of the salvation of men: In the Temple of God the Virgin is clearly seen, and announceth Christ unto all. Let us then cry out aloud to her: Hail, thou fulfillment of the Creator's dispensation."—*Troparion for the day of the Presentation of the Infant Jesus:*—"Hail, Virgin Mother of God, full of grace, for from Thee hath risen the Sun of Righteousness, Christ our God, illumining them that are in darkness. Rejoice thou, also, O righteous Elder, who didst receive into thine arms the Deliverer of our souls, Him that giveth Resurrection unto us."*

Combinations of Daily Services.—In ancient times, especially in monasteries, all the offices of the daily divine service were performed separately, at the hours appointed for them. At the present time they are combined so as to fit into three services: the *evening service*, consisting of the offices of None, Vespers and Complines;—the *morning service*, consisting of the offices of Nocturns, Matins and Prime;—and the *midday service*, consisting of the offices of Terce and Sext and the Liturgy or Mass. On days preceding Sundays or great feast-days, the evening and morning services are joined into one, which is called a *Vigil* (i. e. "keeping awake"), and consists of Vespers, Matins and Prime. As, in some monasteries, this service, beginning after sunset, lasts till daybreak, and always contains the prayers for both evening and morning, it is called *All-night Vigil*.

If a feast-day on which the Liturgy must be performed falls on one of the days in Lent on which no Liturgy is ordered, the following alteration is made in the distribution of the services: The morning service consists of Nocturns, Matins and Prime; the midday service—of Terce, Sext and None, Vespers and the Liturgy, and the evening service—of Complines.

Of the Daily Services.

Vespers begin with the glorification of God, the Creator of the world and its Providence, and consists of the following parts: petitions setting forth our needs; the singing of psalms and an-

---

*The Troparia for the rest of the Twelve Feasts will be found further on, in the chapter on special features of divine service.

thems, expressive of regret for the lost beatitude of Paradise, and repentance of sins; prayers for salvation, and expressions of hope in the Savior. The penitential prayers are followed by a hymn of praise in honor of Christ, who came into the world, then by petitions that the Lord may have mercy on all Christians and grant them spiritual mercies. The service ends with the Lord's Prayer, a hymn of praise in honor of the Mother of God, and the prayer of the Blessed Simeon. Thus the Vesper service is replete with memories of the Creation, the Fall, the expulsion from Paradise and the profound contrition of the best men, who found their only comfort in hope in the Savior and joyfully hailed His coming.

Complines are the prayers before retiring to rest. Sleep being the image of death, this service is permeated with the thought of death, not gloomy, but illumined by the remembrance that Christ, after His death, descended into Hell and brought forth from it the souls of the righteous who awaited His coming. There are the *Great Compline* and the *Little Compline*. The former consists of three parts. In the *first* we give thanks to God for the day and express the hope that He will grant us a restful sleep during the approaching night, and rest after death with the Saints. These feelings find expression, besides all other prayers, in the verse: " God is with us. Understand, ye nations, and submit, for God is with us."—The *second* part is penitential. The substance of all the prayers is expressed in the penitential Troparia* which are sung: " Have mercy on us, Lord, have mercy on us; for we, having no answer to make, offer to Thee, our Master, this one prayer, sinners that we are: Have mercy on us!"—The *third* part of Complines consists in glorifications of the Lord and His Saints. The substance of the prayers composing it is expressed in the Psalm " Praise God in His Saints," with the added anthem: " O Lord of hosts, abide with us, for no

---

*A *Troparion* is a brief hymn on the nature of the event commemorated or on the labors of the person in whose honor the service is performed, also on the meaning of the service. Every service and every day has its own Troparion.

helper have we in our tribulations but Thee only; Lord of hosts, have mercy on us!"—The Little Complines are an abridgment of the Great, consisting of the third part alone. Of the first, only the Creed is read, and of the second the penitential Psalm " Have mercy on me, O God!"

Nocturns are the prayers to be recited at midnight, in memory of Jesus Christ's midnight prayer in the garden of Gethsemane,—in imitation of the angels, who, night and day, glorify the Lord,—and as a reminder that we should be ever ready to give answer on the Day of Judgment to Christ, who will come unexpectedly, as the bridegroom in the night.—The *Daily Nocturns* consist of two parts: The first reminds us by its prayers of the second coming of Christ and the Judgment, proclaiming that " Blessed are the undefiled, who walk in the path of the law of the Lord," while the second part contains prayers for the dead.—The *Sunday Nocturns* consist of glorifications of the Holy Trinity.

Note.—On the days on which an All-night Vigil is ordered, the Complines and Nocturns are omitted.

Matins begin with prayers for the Tsar, and, after these prayers, consist chiefly in praises of the Lord, Who hath given us not daylight alone, but spiritual Light—Christ Savior. Therefore, this entire service is replete with memories of the time when Christ appeared upon the earth, and lived here unrecognized of nearly all men.—The service of Matins is divided into three parts. The *first* part consists in the singing of Psalms expressive of penitence and hope in the Redeemer, and general prayers for mercy. The psalm-singing begins with the Doxology which the angels sang on the night of the Nativity: " Glory to God in the highest, and on earth peace, goodwill toward men;"—then is interrupted by a more direct glorification of the Incarnation of Christ:—" God is the Lord and hath appeared unto us; blessed He that cometh in the name of the Lord,"—and ends with the glorification of the person or event, to the memory of whom or which the day is consecrated.—The *second* part is entirely consecrated to the glorification of the Saint of the day or of the event commemorated on that day. It consists of hymns from the Old Testament, which refer to the coming Savior, and others from the New Testament, showing that the expectations of the righteous men of old have been realized.—The *third* part consists of hymns of praise and prayers for the granting of spiritual gifts to Christians.

Hours, or *Hour offices*, is the name given to brief sets of prayers recited at the hours which begin each of the four watches of the day, and which, to Christians, are associated with special memories. All these offices are alike in their composition. Every Hour begins with an invitation to adore Christ and consists of the reading of three Psalms. Then follow: the Troparion for the day, the *Theotokion* (a hymn in honor of the Mother of God), the Lord's Prayer, the *Condakion** for the day, the prayer "For every time of day, for every hour," and the concluding prayers of the hour. But with all this similarity, the office of one Hour differs from that of another in so far that each Hour has its own Psalms and concluding prayers, to conform with the events commemorated and with the feelings, thoughts and wishes which these memories call forth in the soul of the believer.—The office of the *First Hour* or *Prime* commemorates the bringing of Christ before Pilate; that of the *Third Hour* or *Terce* commemorates Pilate's judgment of Christ, the scourging and the mocking, and the Descent of the Holy Ghost upon the Apostles; the office of the *Sixth Hour* or *Sext* commemorates Christ's going forth to Golgotha, the Crucifixion, the insults offered to Him on the cross, the darkness which covered the earth; while the office of the *Ninth Hour* or *None* commemorates Christ's Passion and death.

The All-Night Vigil.—This is the name of a service composed of Vespers and Matins, which is performed with great solemnity, especially in the parts consecrated to the memories of the day.

---

*The *Condakion* is a short hymn, similar in substance to the Troparion, but differing from it in that it develops more amply some one part of the Troparion, as for instance this or that particular deed of the Saint of the day, or some one feature of the day's feast.

VESPERS.

The Beginning of the Service and the Prœmiac (Prefatory or Introductory) Psalm.—The service begins with the glorification of the Holy Trinity. With the Royal Gates open, the Church being fully illumined, the Priest, standing before the altar, sayeth:—" Glory to the holy, consubstantial, life-giving and undivided Trinity;" then the Deacon* thrice invites the congregation to worship Christ, our God and King. In answer to this invitation, the faithful—or the choir in their stead—proceed to sing Psalm 103 of David, which glorifies God the Creator and His Providence:—" Bless the Lord, O my soul! O Lord, my God, Thou art very great; Thou art clothed with honor and majesty. * * * Marvellous are Thy works, O Lord! in wisdom hast Thou made them all. * * * Glory to Thee, O Lord, who hast created all things!" The Psalm is concluded with the thrice-sung " Alleluia!" which means " Praise the Lord," or " May the Lord be praised!" This Psalm beginning the series of the daily services, it is called *Prœmiac, i. e.,* " prefatory " or " introductory." The words of it induce the worshippers into the blissful condition of the first man, when he, innocent as yet, praised his Creator together with the holy angels. The open Royal Gates remind us that sin did not at that time separate men from God, while the light of the lamps and candles and the fumes of the incense symbolize the Divine Light, which illumined men, and the grace of the Holy Ghost which quickened them.

The Great Ectenia (Suffrages).—After the glorification of the Creator in the words of the Prœmiac Psalm, short petitions for the granting of various favors are slowly recited by the Deacon, and after each petition the worshippers—or the choir in their stead—sing the response " Lord, have mercy! " The collection of these petitions is called *Ectenia,* from a Greek word which means " extended, protracted." It begins with the invitation: " In peace let us pray to the Lord,"(i. e. " *being at peace with all*

---

*If the service is performed without the assistance of a deacon, all that a deacon should do is done by the priest.

men and undistracted in spirit"),—and consists of supplications for the peace that is from above and for the salvation of our souls (*i.e. that the Lord may be at peace with us, forgive us our transgressions and grant through this salvation to our souls*);—" for the peace of the whole world, the good estate of the holy churches of God and the union of them all" (*i. e. that the Lord may grant peace to the whole world, help Christian communities to stand firm in faith and piety, cause the divisions between Christians to cease, and unite them all into one Church*);—"for this holy House (*wherein the service is performed*), and those that with faith, reverence and fear of God enter into it." Then follow supplications for various members of the Church and the State to which we belong: "For the Most Holy Governing Synod" (*i. e. the body of bishops and presbyters or priests who govern the Church*), " for our Bishop N., the honorable Presbytery (*the body of priests generally*), the Diaconate in Christ (the *body of deacons*), and for all the Clergy (*all persons attached to the Church, including readers, choristers, sextons*), and the laity (*the congregation and parishioners*);—for our most pious sovereign, the Emperor, and the entire reigning House (*the Imperial family*), all the Palace (*the functionaries appointed by the Tsar*), and the Army;—" that He may aid them and put down beneath their feet every enemy and adversary," (*i. e. that the Lord may aid them in all things, and subdue their enemies, open or secret, and their adversaries*);—" for this city" (*wherein the Church is*), "for every city and country" (*the whole empire*),"and those that in faith dwell therein"(*i.e. the Christian population*). After offering up petitions for the members of the Church and the State, we pray to the Lord " for wholesomeness of air, for abundance of the fruits of the earth and for peaceful times," (*i. e. that the Lord may deliver us from epidemics, which attack through the air, from bad crops, and from war*);—for them that are at sea, that travel, that are suffering (*from hunger and cold, or from enemies*); that are sick, that are in captivity and for their salvation;—" that we may be delivered from all affliction, wrath, and want;"—that He may " succor us, save us, have mercy on us, and keep us, by His grace." The Ectenia ends by our committing ourselves to the will of God:—" Commemorating our most holy, most pure, most blessed, glorious Lady, the God-bearing ever-virgin Mary, let us commend ourselves, and one another, and all our life, to Christ our God." In response to these words, the worshippers sing " To Thee, O Lord." Upon which, the petitions being ended, the Priest calls out aloud:—" For to Thee are due all glory, and honor, and worship, to the Father, and to the Son, and to the Holy Ghost, now and ever, and unto the ages of the ages;" *i. e. we offer our supplications unto Thee, because to Thee, the Triune God, we owe glory, honor and adoration.* In response to this exclamation of the Priest the worshippers utter the word, " Amen," which means " aye, truly is this so."—This Ectenia is called "the Great," because it consists of many petitions, also " the Ectenia of Peace," because it beseeches for mercy. It is recited in front of the closed Royal Gates, in token that sin has removed us from God and has closed against us the doors of the Kingdom of Heaven. The closing of the Royal Gates soon after the Procemiac Psalm is meant to signify that the bliss of our first parents in Eden was of brief duration.

The Kathismata.—The great Ectenia is followed by the singing or reading of the *Kathismata*. This name is given to sections of the Psalter, that book of the Old Testament in which are collected the Psalms, or sacred songs of the ancient Hebrews.* Each Kathisma is subdivided into three *stases*, and each *stasis* is separated from the next by the thrice repeated singing of " Alleluia," with the addition of the words " Glory to Thee, O God,"—whence the *stases* are also called " Glories." In ancient times all the Kathismata were sung alternately by two choirs; hence the separate parts of them have also been called *Antiphons, i. e.* anthems sung " antiphonally," in alternate, responding parts.† The word " Kathisma " is derived from a Greek word which means " to sit." The sections of the Psalter

---

*The entire Psalter containing 150 Psalms, is divided into 20 Kathismata which are all read in the course of the Services of the week. During Lent the entire book is read through twice in the course of the week.

†At present the evening Kathisma is sung only at Sunday, and feast-day Vespers; on all other days, and almost always at Matins the Kathismata are read and only the " Glories " are sung.

are so called, because, in ancient times, they were followed by homilies, during which the congregation was permitted to sit. At the present time, though the homilies have been suppressed, the name is preserved, because it is permitted to sit during the reading of the Psalms. At Sunday and feast-day Vespers the first Antiphon of the first Kathisma is sung, containing regrets over the happy estate forfeited through sin, together with hopes of salvation. The verses of the Psalms are separated by the singing of "Alleluia:"—"Blessed is the man who walketh not in the council of the ungodly" (Alleluia!) "Serve the Lord with fear and rejoice before Him with trembling." (Alleluia!) "Blessed are all they that put their trust in Him." (Alleluia!) "Arise, O Lord; save me, O my God." (Alleluia!) "Salvation belongeth unto the Lord: Thy blessing is upon Thy people" (Alleluia).

The Little Ectenia.—On the Kathisma follows the Little Ectenia, which is an abridgment of the Great Ectenia. It begins with an invitation to prayer:—"Again and again in peace let us pray to the Lord;" it consists of only one petition: "Help us, save us, have mercy on us, and keep us, O God, by Thy grace," and ends with the commendation to God's will and the Doxology. The Little Ectenia serves to divide one portion of the service from the next.

The Verses of the Psalms, "Lord, I Have Cried," and Their Sticheræ.—Repentance for sins committed calls forth in the human soul entreaty for mercy. Therefore, after the Kathisma, selected verses from the Psalms are read ("O Lord, I have cried unto Thee, hearken to me"), in which are expressed: in the first place, supplication from the bottom of the heart, that the Lord may hearken to our unworthy prayers, help us to keep away from evil and from evil men, and receive us among his elect; in the second place, the assurance that the Lord will hear our prayer. The last verses of the Psalms, in which is expressed the hope of salvation, are sung alternately with anthems composed in honor of the person to whom the service is consecrated, and assuring us that the Lord accepts the prayer of those who love Him. These anthems are called *the Sticherœ to the "Lord, I have cried."* The last of them glorifies the Mother of God and contains the dogma of the Incarnation, whence it has the name of "the Mother of God's Dogmatikon."

"Lord, I have cried unto Thee; hearken to me; attend to the voice of my supplication when I cry unto Thee; hear me, O Lord.—Let my prayer be set forth before Thee as incense, and the lifting of my hands as the evening sacrifice.—Bring my soul out of prison, that I may proclaim Thy name. (*Here follows a Stichera.*) The righteous wait for me until Thou reward me. (*Stichera*). From the morning watch until night let Israel trust in the Lord. (*Stichera*). For with the Lord is mercy, and with Him is plenteous redemption, and He Himself shall redeem Israel (*His chosen people*) from all his iniquities. (*Stichera*). Praise the Lord all ye nations, laud Him, all ye peoples. (*Stichera*). For mighty is His mercy waxed toward us, and the truth of the Lord abideth for ever."—(*The Dogmatikon.*)

Vesper Introit and Doxology.—While the last Stichera (the Dogmatikon) is being sung, the Royal Gates are thrown open, in token that the hopes of the faithful have not been idle and that the Incarnation of the Son of God hath opened to them the doors of the Kingdom of Heaven. At this moment the Priest comes out through the north door, preceded by the Deacon with the censer and the candlebearer with the great candlestick and lighted candle, and, standing before the Royal Gates, gives a blessing in the sign of the cross towards the east. The Deacon exclaims aloud: "Wisdom! Stand up!" The exclamation "Wisdom!" signifies that this entrance expresses the coming into the world of the Savior, as thus: The entrance through the north door instead of the Royal Gates signifies that Christ came in lowliness; the lighted candle and the censer remind us that He brought us the light of truth and the grace of the Holy Ghost; the blessing by the sign of the cross signifies that Christ hath opened to us the entrance into the Kingdom of Heaven by His passion on the Cross. By the exclamation "Stand up!" the Deacon invites the worshippers to stand reverently and decorously. They, having heard in the Dogmatikon the news of the Incarnation of the Son of God, and seeing in the Priest's entrance a symbol of the mercies which we have received through this incarnation, sing a hymn of praise to Christ, as being God. While this hymn is being sung, the Priest enters the sanctuary and stands behind the altar, near the Bema.

"O tranquil light of the holy glory of the immortal Father, the Heavenly, the Holy, the Blessed, O Jesus Christ, we, having reached the setting of the sun, (*i. e. having lived to see the sun set*), having beheld the evening light, sing the Father, the Son and the Holy Ghost, Who are God. Worthy art Thou at all times to be sung by reverent voices, O Son of God, Who givest life; wherefore the world doth glorify Thee."

The Prokimenon.—After the Doxology the *Prokimenon* is recited. (The word means "foremost," "principal," "chief"). This name is given to a short verse, generally selected from the Holy Scriptures, which embodies the meaning of the entire service, and therefore, refers to the chief contents of the prayers, hymns and lessons from Scripture for the day.* From its importance, the Prokimenon is emphatically singled out of the service: The Deacon calls out "Let us attend!" the Priest blesses all present, saying "Peace to all!" to which the worshippers respond, with an obeisance, "And to thy spirit," (*i. e. "we wish the same to thy soul"*); the Deacon once more calls out "Let us attend! Wisdom!" (*i. e. "let us be attentive, for words of wisdom will be spoken"*). The Prokimenon is then sung three times. After which the Royal Gates are closed.

The Parœmiæ.—On certain days, the Prokimenon is followed by the reading of *Parœmiæ*. This word means "parable" or "allegory." In church services the name is given to selected lessons or readings from the Scriptures, principally from the Old Testament, containing the prototype of the commemorated event or a prophecy concerning the same, or else explaining the meaning of the feast, or praising the Saint in whose honor the feast is instituted. Parœmiæ are prescribed for all feast-days except Sundays, and for the days of Lent. They differ as to number. Two or three are mostly read.†

---

*Thus the Prokimenon for Sunday Vespers is: "The Lord reigneth; He is apparelled with majesty."

† More Parœmiæ are prescribed for some days than for others. Thus *five* are read at Vespers before the Annunciation, *eight* on the vigil of Christmas-day, *twelve* on the vigil of the Epiphany, and *fifteen* on the Saturday before Easter Sunday.

The Triple Ectenia and the Ectenia of Supplication.—After glorifying Christ as God, we offer up our petitions in the words of two Ectenias, spoken by the Deacon: in the first we entreat mercy for all Christians, while in the second we specify what mercies we desire for their souls. The former is called the "Triple Ectenia" because "Lord, have mercy!" is sung thrice after each petition. The other is called the "Ectenia of Supplication," because the response to each petition is "Grant, O Lord!"

The Triple Ectenia begins with the invitation: "Let us say with our whole soul, and with our whole mind let us say," and consists of petitions for our Emperor,—for his prosperous rule, the preservation of his life, his peace of mind, happiness, salvation; "that the Lord may specially aid and assist him in all things, and subdue under his feet every foe and adversary; —for the reigning House;—for the most Holy Synod, the local Bishop, and all our brethren in Christ;—for the Christ-loving army;—for the blessed and ever remembered founders of this holy House (*in which the service is performed*), and of all our Christian fathers and brethren that have gone to their rest and lie here (*buried around the church*), and in all other places;—for mercy, life, peace, health, salvation, protection, forgiveness and remission of sins for the servants of God, the brethren of this holy House, (*i. e. the parishioners of the church*), those that bring forth fruit (*who make donations*) and do good work (*i. e. bring gifts for the adorning of the church*) in this holy and most venerable church, that labor (*for the good of the church*), that sing, and for the people that stand here before Thee and await from Thee great and rich mercies." The Priest concludes these petitions by a Doxology, in which he explains that we hope to obtain from God what we ask, because He is "a merciful and a man-loving God."

The Ectenia of Supplication begins with the invitation: "Let us accomplish our prayer unto the Lord," and consists of petitions that the Lord may grant us: "That the whole evening may be perfect, holy, peaceful and sinless;—an Angel of peace, a faithful guide, a guardian of our souls and bodies;—forgiveness and remission of our sins and transgressions;—what is good and profitable for our souls, and peace for the world;—that the remaining part of our life may be spent in peace and repentance;—a Christian end to our life, without pain and shame, peaceful, and a good account of ourselves before the dread judgment-seat of Christ."—In the concluding exclamation the Priest again proclaims that we hope to obtain from God what we ask because He is "merciful and man-loving." "In confirmation of this hope, the Priest, after the conclusion of the Ectenia, blesses the congregation, saying, "Peace to all," whereto the latter responds by the good wish "And to thy spirit." After the Ectenia hymns are chanted in honor and memory of the person or event to which the services of the day are sacred. These hymns are separated by verses taken from various parts of the Scriptures, and are, therefore, called *Stichera on Verses.*

Conclusion of Vespers.—Filled with hope in the Son of God, Who, having become incarnated from the Virgin Mary, gave to those that believed in Him the right to call God their Father, we can retire to rest without fear, even though this rest should pass into that of death. Therefore we conclude our evening prayers with the last prayer of the blessed Simeon, the Lord's prayer, a hymn in praise of the Mother of God, and ask God's blessing, exclaiming: "Be the name of the Lord blessed now and for ever." In reply to this, the Priest blesses the people, saying: "The blessing of the Lord be upon you, by His grace and love toward man, always: now, and ever, and unto the ages of the ages."

Simeon's Prayer.—"Lord, now lettest Thou Thy servant depart in peace, according to Thy word. For mine eyes have seen Thy salvation, which Thou hast prepared before the face of all peoples; a light to lighten the Gentiles and the glory of Thy people, Israel."

The Litê, and the Blessing of the Loaves (Artoklasia).—Sometimes, at an All-night Vigil, towards the end of Vespers, the officiating clergy go forth with censers and candles into the vestibule of the church, there to perform the *Litê.* The word means "earnest supplication." In ancient times this was done in order that the catechumens and penitents who stood in the vestibule might participate in the gladness of the festival. The faithful used to come out with the clergy, to signify their humility and their brotherly love towards those who had sinned. At the present time this custom still survives and serves as a reminder to all Christians that they may have a care to the purity of their souls, which alone makes them worthy to enter into the House of God. The Litê consists chiefly of an Ectenia, recited by the Deacon, "for the salvation of the people,—for the Sovereign and his House,—for the clergy,—for all afflicted Christian souls (*afflicted by sorrow or sin*), desirous of aid,—for the city, the country and all Christians living therein,—for the deceased fathers and brethren,—for deliverance from famine, epidemics, earthquakes, flood, fire, sword, hostile invasion and civil strife." After the Ectenia all present bow their heads and the Priest says a prayer in which he beseeches the Lord to "accept our prayer, to grant us the remission of our transgressions, to chase away from us every foe, to keep our life in peace, to have mercy on us and to save us." In the churches which have no vestibule, the Litê is performed inside the church, by the western entrance.

Note.—In times of public calamities, the Litê is sometimes performed out of doors, on fields, public squares or city halls. For this purpose the clergy comes out bearing crosses, banners and ikons, forming a procession.

After the Litê the clergy, to the singing of verses, return from the vestibule into the church, and stand in the middle of it, before a table on which have been placed five loaves of bread and three vessels, one with wheat, one with grape wine and one with oil. After reading the concluding prayers of the Vesper office, the Priest makes the sign of the cross over the loaves and prays the Lord that He may bless them and multiply them "in the whole world, and sanctify the faithful (Christians), who partake of these gifts."—The service concludes with a blessing to the congregation.—In ancient times, immediately after the blessing of the loaves, a portion of the Epistle was read,* with appro-

---

*The name of "Epistle" is given to that portion of the New Testament which contains the Acts of the Apostles, the Epistles and the Apocalypsis (Revelation).

priate explanations. During this reading all sat, and the deacons distributed to the hearers a piece each of the blessed bread and a cup of the wine, that they might sustain their strength. At the present time, the services being abridged, no food is offered between Vespers and Matins.

MATINS.

"**The Six Psalms.**"—At an All-night Vigil Matins begin immediately after the blessing of the congregation by the Priest. The church is dimly illumined and the Royal Gates are closed, while the Reader utters thrice the Angelic Hymn, which was sung on the night of the Nativity, before dawn: "Glory to God in the highest, and on earth peace, good will toward men,"—then slowly reads six Psalms (3, 37, 62, 87, 102 and 142), in which are expressed alternately the sorrow of a soul repenting of its sins (37, 87 and 142), and hope in the mercy of God and salvation (3, 62 and 102). While the three last Psalms are read, the Priest, standing before the Royal Gates secretly—i. e. inaudibly, to himself,—recites the morning prayers, as the advocate of the people before the Lord.

The Great Ectenia, "God is the Lord," and the Kathismata.—After the Six Psalms, we offer up to God our petitions for the granting of spiritual and bodily mercies in the words of the Great Ectenia, then we sing a hymn of praise to God, Who hath descended to earth for our salvation, a continuation to the Angelic Hymn: " God is the Lord and hath appeared unto us; blessed be He that cometh in the name of the Lord." To this hymn is added the Troparion for the feast, as a reminder of the mercies bestowed upon us through the Incarnation of the Son of God. While the hymn, " God is the Lord," and the Troparion are being sung, the illumination of the church is increased, to signify that Christ, having come, is the Light of the world. The Troparion is followed by the Kathismata in their order, expressing, in the words of the Psalms, our consciousness of our unworthiness before God. In ancient times the Lesson from the Epistle was expounded after the reading of the Kathismata. Now the latter are followed immediately by the Little Ectenia.

This part of the Matins office, consisting of a long continued reading of Psalms, interspersed only with brief Doxologies in honor of Christ's coming into the world, and in memory of the mercies which He brought by His coming, reminds us of the time when Christ already lived on the earth, but was recognized by almost no one, while men went on waiting for His coming and prayed to God for mercy, listening in doubt and perplexity to the news that the Lord had already appeared upon the earth. Consisting, as it does, principally of penitential prayers, this part of the Matins office takes place with the Royal Gates closed.

The Poly-elaion.—The second part of the service, consisting of glorifications of the event or person commemorated on the day, is performed with especial solemnity on the vigils of feast-days. After the Kathismata have been read, with the Royal Gates open, the Psalm " Bless the name of the Lord " is sung, with the response " Alleluia!" after each verse. This Psalm (103), is called *Poly-elaion*, i. e. " of many mercies," also " oil-abounding," because the words " His mercy endureth for ever," are frequently repeated in it, and while it is being sung all the lights are lit. At the same time, in token of reverence and festivity, censing goes on in the whole church.

The Magnification and the Sunday Troparia.—On great feast-days, after the Poly-elaion, before an ikon laid on a lectern in the middle of the church, is sung a short verse *magnifying* the person or event celebrated. On Sundays the Troparia of the Resurrection are substituted for this verse; they speak of the Resurrection of Christ and invite the faithful to worship the Most Holy Trinity. These Troparia are sung with the response " Blessed art Thou, O Lord, teach me Thine ordinances," and end with a hymn in honor of the Mother of God (Theotokion).

" The host of the Angels were amazed seeing Thee numbered among the dead, Thee, O Savior, that didst destroy the might of death, that didst raise Adam together with Thyself, and deliver all from Hell."

"Why do ye mingle the myrrh with pitying tears, O ye women-disciples? said the radiant Angel at the grave to the myrrh-bearing women;—behold the grave and understand: for the Savior is risen from the tomb."

"Very early in the morning the myrrh-bearing women hastened to Thy tomb, lamenting; but the Angel stood before them and said: The time for lamentation is passed; weep not, but go and tell the Resurrection to the Apostles."

"The myrrh-bearing women coming with unguents to Thy tomb, O Savior, wept; but the Angel spake unto them saying: Why do ye think that the living is among the dead? For He, as God, is risen from the tomb."

"Let us worship the Father and His Son also, and the Holy Ghost, the Holy consubstantial Trinity, crying with the Seraphim, Holy, holy, holy art Thou, O Lord."

"In bringing forth the giver of life, Thou, O Virgin, hast delivered Adam from sin, and given joy to Eve instead of sorrow; for them that were fallen from life He hath restored to life, He Who of thee was incarnate, God and Man."

The Matinal Antiphons.—The Magnification or Sunday Troparion and the Little Ectenia are followed by the singing of the *Antiphons*, alternately by two choirs. They are different for every Sunday, up to eight, this being the number of chants or tones.

The following Antiphons are sung more frequently than any others:—

"From my youth many passions have afflicted me; but Thou, O my Savior, defend me and save me.

"Ye that hate Zion* shall be put to shame by the Lord, for ye shall be withered by fire, even as grass.—

"By the Holy Ghost is every soul quickened, and exalted by His purity, and illumined mystically by the Trinal Unity."—

The Gospel Lesson.—After the Antiphons comes the Lesson or reading from the Gospels. In order to arouse the worshippers to attention and reverence, the Deacon calls out "Let us attend!" and thereupon a Prokimenon is sung, which indicates the substance of the coming Lesson or reading, after which the Deacon invites the faithful first to praise God, in the words "Let everything that hath breath praise the Lord," then to pray that "the Lord may make us

---

*Zion—the mountain on which stood the palace of David and the Tabernacle containing the Ark of the Covenant. "Haters of Zion" are the foes of the people of Israel, or, in Christian speech—of Christianity.

worthy to hear the Holy Gospel," and lastly calls out "Wisdom! Stand up!" The Priest then blesses the worshippers and announces from which Evangelist the Lesson will be read. In response to this the worshippers sing "Glory to Thee, our God, glory to Thee!" Just before the reading the Deacon once more invites attention by calling out "Let us attend!" Then the Priest begins the reading, on Sundays in the Sanctuary before the altar, and on feast-days in the middle of the church before the ikon of the feast. The Gospel Lesson is adapted to the event commemorated on each given day. On Sundays the Lessons selected for Matins are those that speak of Christ's Resurrection and His apparition after Resurrection.

Adoration of the Testament or the Ikon and Anointing with Oil.—After the Gospel Lesson, if the day is a feast-day, adoration is paid to the ikon of the feast which is laid on a lectern in the middle of the church; if it is a Sunday, the Testament is brought into the middle of the church. The worshippers reverently meet the sacred Book, as it were Christ Himself, and sing a hymn in honor of Him Who was crucified and rose from the dead. During the singing, the faithful pay reverent obeisance to the sacred Book and press their lips to it, as being the living Word of Christ.

"Having beheld the resurrection of Christ, let us adore the holy Lord Jesus, Who alone is without sin. Thy Cross we adore, O Christ, and Thy holy Resurrection we hymn and glorify. For Thou art our God, we know none other beside Thee, we call on Thy Name. Come, all ye faithful, let us adore the holy Resurrection of Christ, for behold! through the Cross joy hath come unto the whole world. Ever blessing the Lord, we sing of His Resurrection; for having suffered crucifixion, Death by Death He overthrew."

If the loaves were blessed earlier in the service, the brow of the faithful is anointed with oil, with the words: "In the name of the Father, and of the Son, and of the Holy Ghost!" in token that the mercy of God is vouchsafed to them, and as a reminder that the Lord demands from them acts of mercy.

The Adoration of the Testament or ikon ends with a hymn, entreating the Lord to have mercy on us according to His great lovingkindness (Psalm 50), and to the prayers of the

Apostles and of the Mother of God. For the granting of this same mercy the Deacon asks in the prayer " Save, O Lord, Thy people, and bless Thine inheritance."

As the Sunday Troparia, the Magnifications, the Antiphons, and the Gospel Lesson are closely connected with one another and with the verses of the Poly-elaion Psalm, and are given only when that Psalm is sung, this whole portion of the service is sometimes called " Poly-elaion." Thence the expression " a service with the Poly-claion " signifies that at the Matins in question there will be a Lesson or reading from the Gospel.

The Scriptural Odes and the Canon.—After the Poly-elaion, nine *Odes* from Holy Scripture are sung, in which Old Testament worthies expressed their hope in a Savior and their readiness to receive Him. To these Odes are added the nine Canticles of the *Canon*. The word "Canon" signifies "rule," " order," and the name is given to a collection of verses (Troparia) in honor of the event or person commemorated, composed after one definite rule, namely: Each Canon is divided into nine parts called Canticles, each of which consists of several short verses or Troparia. The simultaneous singing of the Scriptural Odes and the Canticles of the Canon proceeds after the following established order: First a verse from an Old Testament Ode is chanted, then a Troparion of the Canon; after that the next verse and the second Troparion, and so forth to the end. As the first Troparion of every canonic Canticle serves as a link between an Old Testament Ode and a New Testament Ode, its contents are always taken from the former. Either the event celebrated in the Old Testament Ode is shown to be the prototype of that of the New Testament, or else single expressions are borrowed from the Old Testament. Hence the first Troparion of each canonic Canticle is called *Irmos* (*i. e.* " link "). The following verses of the canonic Canticle are called *Troparia* (*i. e.* " verses that *turn* "), because, by their metre and tone, they *turn* towards their Irmos and conform to it. After each Canticle of the Canon coupled with the Old Testament Ode, the Irmos is chanted again by two choirs, which, for that purpose, come out into the middle of the church. From this manner of singing, this Irmos is called the *Katabasis* (*i. e.* " descent "—from the Soleas where the choirs are placed).

In order to shorten the service, it is usual to sing only the Canticles of the Canon, omitting the Old Testament Odes, except the ninth, since their contents are found in the Irmos of the Canon. In these Canticles chants are introduced between the Troparia of the Canon—petitions or praises addressed to the person in whose honor the Canon is composed.

The first Old Testament Ode is the song in which Moses gave thanks after the passage of the Red Sea, and the submersion of Pharaoh's army. With this Ode is coupled the Irmos of the first Canticle of the Canon, in which this passage is presented as the prototype of our salvation from sin through the waters of baptism, and Jesus is glorified, Who led us out of death into life, saving us from the abysm of sin, from the slough of iniquity.

The second Old Testament Ode is the song in which Moses exhorted the people before his death. It is sung only in Lent.

The third Old Testament Ode is the song of Hannah, the mother of the Prophet Samuel, in which she gave thanks to God for having taken from her the disgrace of barrenness and given her a son. The Irmos of the third Canticle of the Canon points to this event as a type of men who, having been tainted with sin, but having become Christians, were given the strength to bring forth rich fruits of well-doing, and glorifies God in Hannah's words.

The fourth Old Testament Ode is the song of the Prophet Habakkuk, who, under the guise of the blazing sun rising from behind the forest-clad mountain, symbolizes the coming of Christ. The Irmos of this fourth Canticle of the Canon celebrates the Incarnation of Christ from the Virgin Mary in the words of the Prophet Habakkuk.

The fifth Old Testament Ode is that of the Prophet Isaiah which symbolizes the glorious coming of the Savior as the all-vivifying light which raises the dead to life. The Irmos of the fifth Canticle of the Canon celebrates Christ as the Light which delivers us from the darkness of sin.

The sixth Old Testament Ode is the song of the Prophet Jonah, who was swallowed by the whale, expressing his hope to be saved by God. In the Irmos of the sixth Canticle of the Canon the Prophet Jonah is represented now as the prototype of Christ, risen from the dead on the third day, now as a symbol of the human race, swallowed by the spiritual Beast—the Devil, drowning in the sea of life, in the tempest of sins, and finding in the Savior alone a peaceful harbor, in which mankind is secure from the deep of evil.

The seventh and eighth Old Testament Odes are the songs of the three youths, cast by Nebuchadnezzar into the burning fiery furnace. In these songs they first besought God to forgive their transgressions, then glorified Him for their miraculous preservation. In the Irmi of the corresponding Canticles of the Canon, the deliverance of the three youths is made to symbolize the miraculous incarnation of Christ, and the Savior is glorified in their words.

The ninth Ode is from the New Testament. It is the Song of the Virgin Mary, in which she expresses her joy at her meeting with Elizabeth after the Annunciation: " My soul doth magnify the Lord, and my spirit hath rejoiced in God my Savior." This Ode is coupled with that of Zachariah on the birth of his son John the Precursor. When this Ode is sung, the verses are separated by the chant: " More honorable than the Cherubim, and beyond compare more glorious than the Seraphim, thee who, immaculate, didst bear God the Word, verily the Parent of God (*Theotokos*), thee we magnify."—The Virgin's song is never omitted, except on the great Twelve Feast days, when Magnification is substituted for it. The Irmos of the ninth Canticle of the Canon celebrates the Mother of God and the Incarnation of Christ.

In this manner the Irmi of the Canon celebrate the coming of Christ in the words of the Old Testament saints who awaited it, while the Troparia glorify the Lord in connection with the event or the Saint in whose honor the Canon is composed. The Canon is sung with the Royal Gates closed, because New Testament events are celebrated therein under cover of the Old Testament.

The chanting of the Canon is divided into three parts by reciting the Little Ectenia, after the third, sixth and ninth Odes. With the Canon ends that part of the service which is devoted to commemorating the special features of the day.

Note.—These Ecteniæ are distinguished by differences in the Exclamations uttered by the Priest. The first celebrates God as the Creator and Divine Providence:—" For Thou art our God;" the second—as the Savior: " For Thou art the King of the world and the Savior of our souls;" the third—as King of the whole world, visible and invisible, " For Thee all the hosts of Heaven do praise."

The Psalms of Praise, and the Sticheræ on " Praise Ye."—The third and last part of Matins consists of hymns of praise in honor of the Lord and petitions for the granting of spiritual mercies to all Christians. After the Canon are chanted the Psalms 148, 149 and 150, which invite all God's creatures to praise the Lord, and are, therefore, called the " Psalms of Praise:" " Let everything that hath breath praise the Lord;"—" Praise ye the Lord from the heavens; praise Him in the heights; praise Him, all His angels; praise ye Him, all His hosts."—On Sundays the Deacon calls out before these Psalms are sung: " Holy is the Lord our God," as an invitation to begin the song of praise. Between the verses are sung hymns in honor of the event or person commemorated; these are called *the Sticheræ on " Praise ye."* The Psalms of Praise end with a hymn in honor of the Virgin (*Theotokion*):

At Sunday Matins the following Theotokion is sung:

"Exceedingly blessed art thou, O Virgin Mother of God; for by Him that was incarnate of thee Hell hath been led captive, Adam hath been recalled (*from Hell*), the curse hath been made void, Eve hath been set free, and we have been made alive. Wherefore in praising thee we cry: ' Blessed art Thou, O Christ our God, Who didst so will, blessed art Thou.' "

The Great Doxology.—After the Psalms of Praise with their Sticheræ have been chanted, the Royal Gates are opened, and the Priest calls out " Glory to Thee Who hast shown us the Light," thus inviting the faithful to glorify God for having given us the Light of the spirit—Christ Savior, Who came into the world to illumine mankind, which had theretofore lived in the darkness of superstitions and iniquities. In those places where the All-night's Vigil really lasts all night, and where Matins, being performed separately from Vespers, begin very early, the Priest utters these words at sunrise and thereby invites the faithful to glorify God for the gift not of the spiritual light alone, but also of the material light. In answer to the Priest's invitation, the faithful sing the Doxology which begins with the Angelic Song "Glory to God in the highest, and on earth peace, good will toward men," and ends with the *Trisagion:* "Holy God, holy mighty One, holy immortal One, have mercy on us." This Doxology is called "the Great" to distinguish it from "the Little Doxology," which precedes the Six Psalms.

The Great Doxology:
"Glory to God in the highest and on earth peace, good will toward men.

"We praise Thee, we bless Thee, we worship Thee, we glorify Thee, we give thanks to Thee, because of Thy great glory.—O Lord, King of Heaven, God, Father Almighty,—O Lord, Only-begotten Son, Jesus Christ, and O Holy Ghost!—O Lord God, Lamb of God, Son of the Father, that takest away the sins of the world, have mercy on us! Thou that takest away the sins of the world, accept our prayer!—Thou that sittest at the right hand of the Father, have mercy on us!—For Thou alone art holy, Thou alone art the Lord, O Jesus Christ, unto the glory of God the Father. Amen.

"Every day will I bless Thee and praise Thy name, forever, and unto the ages of the ages.

"Vouchsafe, O Lord, that we may be kept without sin this day.—Blessed art Thou, O Lord, God of our fathers, and praised and glorified is Thy name unto the ages. Amen.

"Let Thy mercy, O Lord, be upon us, for we have put our trust in Thee.

"Blessed art Thou, O Lord; teach me Thine ordinances. (*Thrice.*)

"O Lord, our refuge hast Thou been from generation unto generation. I have said: O Lord, have mercy on me, heal my soul, for I have sinned against Thee.—O Lord, unto Thee I fled; teach me to do Thy will, for Thou art my God;—for in Thee is the fountain of life; in Thy light shall we see light (*i. e. 'through knowing Thy teaching we shall learn the truth'*). Oh continue Thy mercy to them who know Thee.

"Holy God, Holy Strong One, Holy Immortal One, have mercy on us."

End of Matins and Prime (Office of the First Hour).—Having celebrated the glory of God, we offer up petitions for all Christians and ask for spiritual mercies in the words of the Triple

Ectenia and the Ectenia of Supplication, after which the Dismissal is made.

After the Vigil is concluded the office of the First Hour is read, which ends with a hymn in honor of the Virgin (*Theotokion*):—

"We thy servants, O Mother of God, sing unto thee hymns of victory, as to our Commander and helper in the strife,—and hymns of thanksgiving, as being delivered by thee from evils. And do thou still, as possessed of might unconquerable, deliver us from all evils, that we may call unto Thee: Rejoice, O Bride unwed!"

NOTE.—Wherein the Daily Services of Vespers and Matins differ from the same Services as performed at an All-night's-Vigil.—The daily Vesper service differs from that performed at a feast-vigil in the following points: 1. The Procœmiac Psalm is read with the Royal Gates closed, not open; 2. the Kathismata are read right along, without the chanted Alleluia after each verse; 3. there is no Vesper or evening Introit, but the hymn "O tranquil light" is recited or sung quickly, with the Royal Gates closed; 4. the Parœmiæ are omitted (excepting in Lent), so are the Litês and the Blessing of the Loaves.—The Vespers service is followed by the Little Compline.

The daily Matins service begins with prayers for the Tsar, consisting of two Psalms, two Troparia, a Theotokion, and an abridged Triple Ectenia. All these contain petitions that the Lord may, through the intercession of the Mother of God, save the Tsar, and grant him victory over all enemies. In the further order of the daily Matins service there are the following differences from the same service as performed at a feast-vigil: 1. There is no Poly-eleion or Gospel Lesson, and immediately after the Kathismata is read Psalm 50, "Have mercy on me, O Lord!"—(the "*Miserere*"),—which is followed by the Scriptural Odes and the Canon; 2. The Great Doxology is recited, not chanted; 3. after the Ectenia, Dismissal is not made, but the reading of Prime begins at once. When Matins are performed apart from Vespers, they are preceded by Nocturns (midnight office).

THE LITURGY.

General Notions on the Liturgy.

In ancient times the name of "liturgy" was given to any common business conducted on a community's contributions. Christians very early came to give the name to that church service during which the Sacrament of the Eucharist is performed, and which is entirely pervaded with memories of the life of Christ Savior from His nativity to His ascension to Heaven,— because at this service gifts are offered to God which have been contributed by the Christian community. It is also called the *Eucharisty* (*i. e.* "Thanksgiving"), because it expresses our gratitude to Christ for our salvation, and again by a Russian word, *obiédnia*, from the fact that it is celebrated before the noonday meal, *obiéd*. In English there is no objection to give the Eucharistian service the generally used name of *Mass*.

The Sacrament of the Eucharist was instituted by Jesus Christ Himself. At the Last Supper He gave Communion to His disciples, making them partake of His Body and Blood under the guise of bread and wine, and commanded them to do this in memory of Him. The Apostles held this commandment of their Master and Lord sacred. When they met together, they spent the time in prayer, in the singing of sacred hymns, and the *breaking of bread* in memory of Christ, i. e. they celebrated the Sacrament of the Eucharist.—Already in the Apostles' time the main order of the prayers and rites of the Liturgy was established among the Christians by oral tradition. In the IV-th century, A. D., the service of the Liturgy was written down by St. Basil the Great, Archbishop of Cæsarea in Cappadocia, and by St. John Chrysostom ("the Golden-Mouthed"), Archbishop of Constantinople, as it was performed in their time, with the addition of several prayers, composed by these prelates. Very few new hymns entered subsequently into the Liturgy. In this manner it came to pass that there are two liturgical rites: the rite of St. John Chrysostom and that of St. Basil the Great; but they are very nearly identical.

The Liturgy being a service connected with a Sacrament, not only the order of it is strictly prescribed, but also the choice of celebrants, the time and place of celebration.

The Liturgy can be celebrated only by a bishop or a priest; and neither a bishop nor a priest may celebrate more than one Liturgy in one day. The celebrant must necessarily take holy communion himself, and for that act he must prepare himself.

The Liturgy can be celebrated only in a church, at an altar on which there is an Antimins consecrated by a bishop. (See p. 11.) Not more than one Liturgy may be celebrated at one altar, with one Antimins, in one day.

The time appointed for the celebration of the Liturgy is, by ancient custom, the ninth hour of the morning. It may sometimes begin either earlier or later, but never earlier than daybreak, nor later than noon, except on the days when the Liturgy is combined with the Vesper service.

The service of the Liturgy is divided into three parts: in the first the elements for the Sacrament are prepared; in the second, the worshippers prepare to take part in the celebration of the Sacrament; in the third, the Sacrament itself is performed.

1. THE PROSKOMIDÉ.

The first part of the Liturgy is named *Proskomidé*, which means "the bringing of gifts." It is so named because, in ancient times, the elements of the Sacrament of the Eucharist were selected out of the voluntary offerings of the Christians, while at the present time they are purchased for money contributed by Christians. It is performed by a priest, robed in the full vestments of his dignity.

The elements of the Sacrament are bread and wine. The bread must be made of wheat flour, mixed with plain water, leavened, well baked, fresh and clean, neither musty nor stale. These loaves are called *prosforá*, i. e. "oblations." Each consists of two smaller round loaves superposed, indicating that in Jesus

Christ two natures are united, the divine and the human. On the top of each loaf there is a cross, with the following Greek inscription in the four corners: IC. XC. HI. KA., signifying "Jesus Christ prevails." Five loaves are used in the preparation of the Sacrament.—The wine must be made of the juice of the grape, without admixture, not sour nor sharp, not mildewed nor yet rancid.

Taking up the first loaf, the Priest makes the sign of the cross on it with the lance, saying, "In memory of our Lord, and God, and Savior, Jesus Christ;" then he cuts out a cube of the size of the entire stamp, uttering at the same time the words of the Phophet Isaiah, in which he speaks of the Savior as of a Lamb Which takes on Itself the sins of the world. The portion is called the Lamb, and represents Christ, of whom the Paschal Lamb was the prototype. The priest lays the Lamb in the middle of the paten, makes an incision on it in the form of a cross, remembering that Christ also, like unto a Lamb, offered Himself as a sacrifice for the sins of the whole world, then pierces it with the lance, remembering the words of the Gospel: "One of the soldiers pierced His side and straightway there came out blood and water." With the last words he pours wine and water into the chalice.—Out of the second loaf of holy bread the Priest takes a small particle in honor and memory of the Mother of God, and lays it on the paten at the right of the Lamb; this loaf is called "the Mother of God's."—Out of the third loaf he takes nine particles, in honor of the various hosts of saints, who have been found worthy of an habitation in Heaven, with the nine orders of angels, wherefore this loaf is called "the Prosforá of the Nine Orders." The particles taken out of it are placed in three rows at the left of the Lamb.—Out of the fourth loaf, called "the Prosforá of Health," particles are taken, with a prayer for the health of living members of the

THE LAMB AND THE PARTICLES AS ARRANGED ON THE PATEN.

Church and are laid below the Lamb; while lower still, under the " health particles " are placed those taken out of the fifth loaf, which is called " the Requiem-Prosforá," with a prayer for the dead.

Having laid the particles on the paten, the Priest covers them with the asterisk, so as to keep them in the order in which they were laid, and, in doing so, remembers the star which stopped over the house in Bethlehem, wherein the Infant Jesus dwelt. Then the priest covers the paten and the chalice with the veils and the aër in token that Christ, from the first moment of His coming into the world clothed Himself with glory, that His glory covers the whole world, that He covers us also with His grace.

Thus the rites of the Proskomidé commemorate the Nativity of Jesus Christ, Who, from the first moment of His incarnation, was the Lamb destined to be sacrificed for the sins of men, and at the same time the King, Who gathered the believing around Himself as subjects;—we are reminded that, notwithstanding His seeming humiliation, the Divine glory covered Him and shone forth as a star.

Having prepared the elements of the Sacrament, the Priest prays, swinging the censer, that the Lord may bless the gifts (elements) and accept them in memory of those who offered them and of those on whose behalf they were offered, and that He may keep him, the priest, worthy to celebrate the Holy Mystery.

2. THE LITURGY OF THE CATECHUMENS.

Meaning of the Liturgy of the Catechumens, Its Component Parts and Its Beginning.

The second part of the Liturgy is named " the Liturgy of the Catechumens," because not the faithful alone may be present at it, i. e. those who have received baptism, but also the Catechumens, who are preparing for baptism, and the penitents, *i. e.*

such Christians as are, for their sins, excluded from holy communion for a time. This part of the Liturgy consists only of prayers, hymns in honor of the Most Holy Trinity, and readings from the Word of God.

It begins with a glorification of the Kingdom of the Most Holy Trinity, that Kingdom of truth and peace which Jesus came to establish on earth. Then the Great Ectenia, or Ectenia of Peace, is recited, in which we pray that the Lord may give us His peace from above, without which the Kingdom of Heaven may not be entered, and " pacify " the lives of all men on earth.

The Typical Psalms and the Antiphons.—Having besought the mercy of the Lord, we sing hymns treating of the greatest of all His mercies,—the Incarnation of the Son of God. These hymns are sung alternately by two choirs, whence they are called Antiphons. They are divided by two Little Ecteniæ into three parts, in honor of the Most Holy Trinity. To the second Antiphon is always added a hymn in honor of the incarnate Son of God:—" O Only-begotten Son and Word of God, Who art immortal, yet didst deign, for our salvation, to become incarnate of the Holy Parent of God and ever-virgin Mary, without conversion becoming man" (*becoming man without ceasing to be God*); and wast crucified, O Christ God, overcoming death by death, being one of the Holy Trinity (*one of the persons of the Holy Trinity*), glorified together with the Father and the Holy Ghost—save us."

Antiphons are of various kinds. On Sundays and feast-days Psalms 102 and 145 are sung; they are called " Typical Antiphons," because they are typical of the mercy of God to man.

Verses from Psalm 102:—"Bless the Lord, O my soul, and all that is within me bless His holy name.—Bless the Lord, O my soul and forget not all His benefits.—Who cleanses all thy iniquities; Who healeth all thy diseases; Who redeemeth thy life from corruption; Who crowneth thee with lovingkindness and mercies; Who satisfieth thy desire with good things . . . The Lord is merciful and gracious, long suffering and plenteous in mercy . . ."

Verses from Psalm 145 (Second Antiphon):—"Praise the Lord, O my soul. While I live will I praise the Lord; I will sing praises unto my God while I have any being . . ."

When these Psalms are sung, the Beatitudes take the place of the third Antiphon. This is the name given to Christ's sayings about them that are blessed, combined with the Troparia of the daily or feast-day Canon.—On great feast-days the Antiphons consist of prophetic verses selected from Psalms appropriate to the festive event, and to them are joined hymns indicating the nature of the feast.

The Introit with the Gospel.—Immediately after the hymns in honor of the Holy Trinity, the faithful are prepared for the Lessons from the Scriptures. In the old times of persecution, the holy Book was brought out of the repository for the sacred vessels, which was in a secret place. This custom has been preserved as a memorial of the old usage and as an allusion to Christ's coming and bringing the preaching of the Gospel into the world. The Deacon opens the Royal Gates and brings out, through the northern door, the Testament which lies on the altar, preceded by a candle-bearer and followed by the Priest. The lighted candle indicates that the Word of God is light to our spirit, that the Law of God consecrates the path of our life, and that we are expected to harbor the light of faith and the warmth of love, without which the teaching of Christ would be as unintelligible to us as is the instruction of parents to children who do not love them or believe in them. Standing before the Royal Gates, the Priest gives a blessing towards the East, with the words: " Blessed is the entrance of Thy Saints, O Lord;" then the Deacon calls out: " Wisdom. Stand up!" alluding to the wisdom which is contained in the meaning of this Introit, and inviting reverent attention. On great feast-days, this is followed by a short verse from the Psalms, containing a prophecy concerning the commemorated event. In the Book of the Gospel the faithful see Christ Himself, Who came into the world to preach His doctrine, and adore Him by singing the solemn hymn: " Come, let us worship, and fall down to Christ. O Son of God, Save us, who sing to Thee 'Alleluia.' " Then are sung the Troparion and the Kondakion for the day or feast, in which are pictured the mercies bestowed on us by the coming of the Savior.

The Trisagion.—The Priest concludes the Troparion and the Kondakion by the exclamation: "For holy art Thou, our God, and to Thee we send up glory," thus inviting the worshippers to celebrate the Holy Trinity; to which the worshippers respond by singing the Trisagion: "Holy God, holy Strong One, holy Immortal One, have mercy on us." When the celebrant is assisted by a deacon, the Trisagion is brought out with greater emphasis. After the Kondakion the Deacon asks a blessing of the Priest: "Bless, Master, that we may sing the Trisagion," and having received the blessing, at the exclamation "For holy art Thou, our God," turns round and faces the people, saying "Lord, save the pious and hearken unto us." The choir repeats this petition, then sings the Trisagion.

On the days of the Nativity of Christ, of the Epiphany, on Lazarus' Saturday and Holy Saturday, during the Paschal week and on the day of Pentecost, the following words are sung instead of the Trisagion: "Those who have been baptized in Christ, are clothed with Christ. Alleluia." The reason for this substitution is that, in ancient times, catechumens were wont to receive the sacrament of baptism preferably on those days. The Church has preserved the custom in order that we, who have received baptism, may be mindful of the pledges we then gave. On the day of the Exaltation of the Cross (14th of September) and on the third Sunday in Lent, consecrated to the adoration of the Cross, the following is sung in place of the Trisagion: "Thy Cross we adore, O Master, and we glorify Thy holy Resurrection."

The Reading of Lessons from the Epistle and the Gospel.—After the singing of the Trisagion, the celebrants retire to the Bema. A Bishop stands on the Bema itself; a Priest behind the altar next to the Bema. At the same time the Reader comes out into the middle of the church bearing the Epistle and recites a Prokimenon. In order to call the hearers' attention to it, as being a verse which indicates the substance of the Lesson, the Deacon exclaims, "Let us attend," after which the Priest blesses the people, wishing them peace, and the Deacon exclaims, "Wisdom!" After the Prokimenon, the Reader announces out of what book he is going to read, and the Deacon once more invites attention, exclaiming, "Let us attend." Then begins the reading of the Lesson for the day.

The reading of the Epistle is followed by that of the Gospel, i.-e. of the Lesson for the day out of one of the four evangelists. The worshippers are prepared also for the attentive hearing of the Gospel Lesson. First "Alleluia" is solemnly chanted, it having the same signification as the Prokimenon before the Epistle. Only on Holy Saturday the following Prokimenon is substituted for the "Allelulia:" " Rise, O God, and judge the earth, for Thou inhabitest in all the nations." During the chanting of the "Alleluia," the censer is swung in allusion to the grace of God vouchsafed through His Word. Then the Priest exclaims, " Wisdom ! Stand up ! Let us hearken to the holy Gospel," and blesses the people, wishing them peace, and the Deacon announces from which Evangelist the Lesson is taken. The worshippers give expression to their heartfelt joy by chanting, " Glory to Thee, our God, glory to Thee." The Priest repeats his invitation, "Let us attend," and the Deacon reads the Gospel Lesson. After which " Glory to Thee, our God, glory to Thee," is sung again, and the Royal Gates are closed.

Common Prayers for the Members of the Church and Departure of the Catechumens.—After hearing the word of Christ Savior all present offer up prayers for all the members of the Church, living or dead, in the words of the Triple Ectenia. If, in the first part of the Liturgy, oblations were offered in memory of the dead, a special Requiem Ectenia is then recited. If the service includes prayers for deliverance from national disasters, such as an epidemic, famine, war, or for the deliverance of some particular Christian from sickness, from accidents while traveling, and the like, these petitions are added to those of the Triple Ectenia. These common prayers are followed by the special Ectenia for the Catechumens, in which we pray that the Lord may " Teach them the Word of Truth—reveal to them the Gospel of Righteousness,—unite them to His Church; that He may save them, have mercy on them, succor them and keep them by His grace, so that they also may, together with us, glorify His most pure and majestic Name."

Immediately after these prayers follows the departure of the Catechumens. The Deacon repeatedly exclaims, "As many as are Catechumens, depart." In ancient times the prayers of the faithful began only after the deacons had ascertained that none of the Catechumens remained in the church. At the present time, when baptism is usually administered in infancy, there seldom are any Catechumens in a church, consequently the "departure of the Catechumens" takes place rarely and not everywhere. But the allusion is preserved in the service, to remind the faithful of the vows they took at baptism, and arouse in them a humble consciousness of sin.

3. THE LITURGY OF THE FAITHFUL.

What the Liturgy of the Faithful represents and the principal acts which compose it.—The third part of the Liturgy is named "The Liturgy of the Faithful," because none but the faithful may be present at the celebration thereof,—*i. e.* such persons as have received the Sacrament of Baptism and endeavor to live in accordance with the Christian law.

After the Catechumens have left the church, the Deacon calls out, "As many as are of the Faithful, again and again, in peace let us pray to the Lord," and with this invitation to prayer opens the Liturgy of the Faithful, in the course of which Christians call to mind the passion, death, burial, resurrection, ascension and second coming of Christ Savior, and pray that the Lord may accept their gifts and make them partakers in His Last Supper. The order of the prayers and rites of the Liturgy is disposed to correspond with these memories and petitions.

The Liturgy of the Faithful is divided into four parts: (*a*) The final preparation of the Elements and the faithful for the Sacrifice; (*b*) the offering of the Sacrifice, *i. e.* the performance of the Sacrament and commemoration of the members of the Church; (*c*) the preparation for Communion and the partaking of Communion and (*d*) thanksgiving for Communion and the conclusion of the service.

(A.) Preparation of the Elements and the Faithful for the Sacrifice.

The Great Introit.—After the two Little Ecteniæ for the faithful have been recited, ending with the exlamation, "Wisdom!" the Royal Gates are opened and the choir sings the hymn on the transfer of the Elements to the altar, which hymn is called the *Cherubic Hymn*, because we are preparing to minister at the Throne of God on earth even as the Cherubim minister at the Heavenly Throne.

The Cherubic Hymn.—" Let us, that are mystically representing the Cherubim and singing unto the life-giving Trinity the thrice-holy hymn, now put away all the cares of this life; that we may worthily receive the King of all, who is invisibly escorted* by the Angelic Orders. Alleluia. Alleluia. Alleluia."

While the Cherubic Hymn is sung, after censing with incense, the solemn transfer of the Elements from the Table of Oblations to the altar takes place. In the middle of the hymn, immediately after the words "put away all the cares of this life," the singing is interrupted; at this moment the celebrants—the Deacon holding the paten poised on his head, the Priest holding the chalice in his hands, both preceded by candlebearers—come out of the northern door, and, stopping before the Royal Gates, with their faces to the people, pray first for the Emperor and his House, then for the Most Holy Synod, the local bishop and all Orthodox Christians, "that the Lord may remember them in His Kingdom." When mentioning the members of the Church, the celebrants also mention on whose behalf and with what petitions the Sacrifice is to be offered. Then, entering the sanctuary by the Royal Gates, the Priest places the paten and

---

*The word used in Greek and in Old-Slavic means literally "borne on lances" and alludes to the ancient military custom of soldiers raising their general on their shields above the points of their lances, and carrying him thus surrounded by troops, so that, from a distance, it looked as though he were borne on the points of lances.

the chalice upon the unfolded Antimins, while the Deacon closes the Royal Gates and draws the curtain behind it, in memory of the burial of Christ, Who received death for our sins. During this time the choir ends the Cherubic Hymn.

Christians reverently receive the Elements brought out to them, vividly recalling Christ as He, of His own free will, goeth forth to suffering and death, and pray, in the words of the penitent thief, "that He may remember them all also in His Kingdom."*

Petition for Spiritual Mercies, Exhortation to Love and Peace, and Profession of Faith.—After the Cherubic Hymn follows the Ectenia of Supplication, in which, putting away all worldly care, we ask for spiritual mercies only. To the petitions of this Ectenia is added a petition "for the precious Gifts that have been offered."

After the Ectenia the faithful are reminded of the things which are demanded of each of them in order that the Sacrifice which they offer may be acceptable to God: spiritual peace, mutual love, and unity of faith. The Priest, as he blesses the people, says "Peace to all;" to which they reply "And to thy spirit." Then the Deacon exclaims: "Let us love one another, †)that we may with one mind confess"—when the choir in the name of all present announces Who is to be confessed: "the Father and the Son and the Holy Ghost, the Trinity consubstantial and undivided;" after which they chant the profession of faith, the Creed or "Symbol of Faith."—"I believe in one God, the Father Almighty.". . . As faith reveals to us the mysteries of the Deity and proclaims the resurrection of Christ, Who ac-

---

*Notwithstanding the reverence with which Christians should receive the Elements at the Great Introit, the Church regulations forbid prostrations at this moment, that infidels may have no occasion to say that Christians adore bread and wine as they do God.

†In ancient times the faithful, at these words, embraced and kissed, with the mutual greeting: "Christ is in our midst"—"He is and will be." But in the course of time not all preserved the Christian brother-love; besides, many forgot that Christ is in their midst at this moment; so the ancient custom is now dispensed with, and is observed only by the celebrants at the altar.

cepted death on the cross for our sakes, the curtain is drawn away at this moment, as the seal from the grave, the veil is lifted from the Elements, and the Priest fans them with it from above, symbolizing the breath of the grace of the Holy Ghost. In the East this act of fanning the Elements was originally instituted and is maintained to this day, as a protection against dust and insects. In ancient times the Christians did not reveal the mysteries of their faith to Pagans and Jews, therefore, before the chanting of the Creed, the Deacon called to the doorkeepers "The doors! the doors!" ordering them to look out sharply that no unbaptized intruder might enter, then turned to those present with the words, "in wisdom let us attend." At the present time, when there is no need of guarding the church doors, these words are uttered by the Deacon as a reminder to the worshippers that they should guard the doors of their souls, and not admit into it any thoughts, wishes or feelings unworthy of the holiness of the great Sacrament.

Invitation to Attend.—When the worshippers have ended their profession of faith, which entitles them to be present at the Liturgy of the Faithful, the Deacon invites their reverent attention, so they may worthily offer the sacrifice to the Lord:—"Let us stand well; let us stand with awe; let us attend to offer in peace the holy sacrifice." The choir responds for the faithful, telling in what their sacrifice shall consist: "A gracious peace (*of spirit*), a sacrifice of praise." Then the Priest blesses their intention, saying: "The grace of our Lord Jesus Christ and the love of God the Father and the Communion of the Holy Ghost be with you all." The faithful receive this blessing with bowed heads, in token of reverence, and respond, "And with thy spirit." The Priest once more invites the faithful to attend closely and to keep free of all earthly things: "Let us lift up our hearts!" to which the faithful respond "We have them with the Lord." With this ends the preparation for the Sacrament of the Eucharist.

(B.) THE CONSUMMATION OF THE SACRAMENT.

The Prayer of Thanksgiving, the Offering and Consecration of the Gifts.—The consummation of the Sacrament begins with the Priest's exclamation: "Let us give thanks to the Lord." The faithful, in response to this invitation, adore the Lord, and, mindful of all His mercies, sing the hymn: "Meet and right it is to adore the Father, and the Son, and the Holy Ghost, the Trinity consubstantial and undivided." In order that the absent also may, at this solemn instant of the service, join their prayers of thanksgiving to those of the faithful in the church, the bells are set tolling (in single-strokes). After adoring the Holy Trinity, the Priest lifts the asterisk from the paten, and invites the people to express their thanksgiving to the Lord not only by adoration, but also by singing the triumphal hymn in His honor: "Singing, vociferating, crying and saying the triumphal hymn" (*i. e* "*let us give thanks to the Lord, singing a triumphal hymn to Him with all the powers of our souls*";*) and the faithful, in response to this invitation, sing the triumphal hymn composed of the song of the Angels who surround the Throne of God in heaven, and that with which the Jews met Christ on the occasion of His festive entrance into Jerusalem: "Holy, holy, holy is the Lord Sabaoth (Lord of hosts), Heaven and earth are filled with Thy glory!—Hosanna in the highest!—Blessed is He Who cometh in the name of the Lord! Hosanna in the highest!"—†

Having rendered thanks to God for all His mercies by adoration and song of praise, the Priest utters the words, in which

---

*The words "singing, vociferating, crying and saying" mean that we should sing the glory of God jointly with those higher angels who surround the throne of God—those angels whom the Prophet Ezekiel saw in his vision, in the shape of four animals having each four faces: an eagle's, a bull's, a lion's and a man's. As these faces are merely symbols of the spiritual qualities or forces of the angels, the praise uttered in the voices of the four angelic faces is a praise uttered with all the forces of the soul.

†*Hosanna* is a Hebrew word which means "God save" or "help." "Hosanna in the highest" means either "Hosanna to the Most High," or "May our good wishes be heard in the highest abodes (in Heaven)."

Christ instituted the Sacrament of the Eucharist, which is the greatest monument of God's supreme love for men: "Take, eat (*the bread*); this is my body which is broken for you unto the remission of sins"; and " drink ye of it (*the cup*); this is my blood of the New Testament,* which is shed for you and for many, unto the remission of sins." The faithful calling to mind at these words the Last Supper, the passion and death of Christ, respond "Amen."

Then the Priest, in fulfillment of Christ's command, to " do this in memory of Him," raises the paten and the chalice, saying as he does so: " Thine own, from Thine own we offer in behalf of all and for all" (*i. e.* "*What is Thine own we offer from Thine own servants in behalf of all men, and for all Thy mercies*"); and the faithful, taking up his words, chant: " Thee we hymn, Thee we bless, to Thee we give thanks, O Lord, and to Thee, our God, we pray." While this hymn is being chanted, the Priest prays that the Lord may send down His Holy Spirit on the offered Gifts, consecrate them, and transmute the bread into His true Body, and the wine into His true Blood, then blesses the Gifts. At this instant, by the might of God, the bread and the wine are *transubstantiated* into the Body and Blood of Christ. All who are present in the Church express their veneration for the sacred Mystery by a prostration.

Commemorating the Members of the Church.—After the consecration of the elements, the Priest commemorates the members of the Church, in whose behalf they have been offered. He says in his prayer that we offer this sacrifice for all the Saints who have gone to their rest (*i. e. died*)—more especially for the Mother of God—and that we beseech Him, that, hearing their prayers, He may visit us and be mindful of all those who have died in the hope of a resurrection. The Deacon at the same time reads the Diptychs, or Remembrancer

---

*The blood of the Old Testament is the blood of animals, which were offered in sacrifice and were the prototype of Christ. But the blood of the New Testament is the Blood of Christ, shed for our salvation. Because the wine offered at the Liturgy is mystically transmuted into the blood of Christ, therefore the New Testament sacrifice is called "the Bloodless Sacrifice."

—*i. e.* lists of names of deceased Christians. After praying for the dead, the Priest prays for the living—that the Lord may be mindful of the Bishops, the Priests, of all Christian people, of the Emperor and his House, of the Palace and the Army. This commemoration of the members of the Church the Priest begins while the choir is singing, "To Thee, our God, we pray." When this prayer is ended he commemorates aloud the Mother of God: "Particularly we entreat Thee for our most holy, most pure, most blessed, glorious Lady the Parent of God (*Theotokos* in Greek), and ever-Virgin Mary." To this prayer the faithful respond with a hymn of praise in honor of the Mother of God: "Meet it is, indeed, to call thee blessed." On great feast-days, the choir sings in the place of this hymn, the Irmos of the ninth Ode of the morning Canon. While the hymn "Meet it is" is being sung, the priest proceeds with the commemoration of the members of the church; and when it is ended he commemorates aloud, of the living, the bishops, as the governors and pastors of the Church: "Among the first be mindful, O Lord, of the Most Holy Synod (*the council of bishops*), and our bishop, * * * whom preserve unto Thy holy churches in peace, safety, honor; let them attain to length of days, and rightly impart the Word of Thy truth." The Deacon, during this time, reads the list of the living who are to be commemorated.

The Priest ends the commemoration of the members of the Church with the prayer: "And grant us, (*i. e. help us—all that have been commemorated, together with the Saints and all who have died in the hope of resurrection*), with one mouth and one heart to glorify and hymn Thine all-honorable and majestic Name—of the Father and the Son and the Holy Ghost, now, and ever, and unto the ages of ages."—The worshippers respond "Amen!" in token of their participation in the offering of the Sacrifice and in the commemoration of the members of the Church. This part of the Liturgy of the Faithful also concludes with the Priest's blessing: "And the mercies of the great God and of our Savior Jesus Christ be with you all," and with the worshippers wishing the Priest the same mercies: "And with thy spirit."

(C.) The Preparation for Communion and the Act of Communion.

The Preparation of the Faithful for Communion.—Immediately after the commemoration of all the members of the Church, begins the preparation of the faithful for Communion. The Deacon recites the Ectenia of Supplication, which he begins with the invitation: "Having commemorated all the Saints, again and again in peace let us pray to the Lord," to which he adds a petition for the precious gifts offered, and consecrated," that the Lord accepting them at His holy, heavenly and spiritual altar (*i. e. unsubstantial, not like the material altar erected by us*), as the odor of a spiritual sweet smell, may in return send down to us the divine grace and the gift of the Holy Spirit and deliver us from all affliction, wrath and necessity." The Ectenia concludes with the Priest's praying that the Lord may vouchsafe to let us address Him uncondemned as our Father, in the Lord's Prayer: "And vouchsafe, O Master, that we may with boldness, uncondemned, dare to call upon Thee, God, the Heavenly Father, and say "Our Father which art in Heaven," etc. The Lord's Prayer is then chanted by the faithful (the choir). Then the Priest gives them his blessing with the good wish "Peace be with you," and the Deacon invites them to bow down their heads before the Lord. At this moment the curtain is drawn; the priest, after the Deacon's exclamation "Let us attend" elevates the consecrated Lamb, saying: "the Holy to the holy!" (*i. e. the holy gifts can be offered only to those who are holy.*) All present, with profound veneration, adore with a prostration the Holy Lamb, and say in the consciousness of their unworthiness: "One only is holy, One only is the Lord Jesus Christ, unto the glory of God the Father. Amen."

The Preparation of the Elements for Communion and the Communion of the Celebrants.—After the faithful have been prepared for receiving holy communion, the Priest breaks the Lamb in four parts, saying: "Broken and distributed is the

Lamb of God, which is broken yet not severed, which is ever eaten yet never consumed, but sanctifies those who participate," —and places these parts on the paten in the shape of a cross. Then he places one portion in the chalice with the words: "The consummation of the Holy Spirit," (meaning that *the Sacrament is consummated through the action of the Holy Spirit*); then he blesses the warm water, saying: "Blessed is the warmth (*i. e. the warmth of heart*) of Thy Saints," and pours some into the chalice, saying: "The warmth of faith is full of the Holy Spirit" (*i. e. the warmth of faith is enkindled in the human soul through the action of the Holy Spirit*). Uniting the Body and Blood of Christ, the Priest remembers the resurrection of Christ from the dead, and, by the words uttered at that moment, indicates that the Sacrament is consummated through the action of the Holy Spirit, that only one possessed of warm faith may participate in this Sacrament, and that this faith is enkindled in the human soul by the grace of the Holy Spirit.

After all these acts have been performed, the celebrants take communion, partaking first of the Body, then of the Blood of Christ, after which the remaining portions of the Lamb are dropped into the chalice, the Sunday hymns being recited the while. If there are no communicants (*i. e. no persons duly prepared to receive holy communion*) all the portions taken out of the oblation-loaves in honor of the Virgin and the Saints, and in memory of the dead and the living, are now dropped into the chalice, with the prayer, "Cleanse, O Lord, the sins of those here commemorated, by Thy precious Blood and by the prayers of Thy Saints." If there are communicants, these portions remain in the paten until wanted.

During the act of breaking the Lamb, of uniting the Elements, and of communion by the celebrants, a hymn is sung, which is called "the Communion Hymn," and which relates to the memories of the day and the Lessons from the Gospels and the Epistle. The communion hymn for Sunday is, "Praise God in Heaven, praise Him in the highest. Amen." This hymn is usually followed by the sermon or homily.

The Communion of Laymen.—After the communion hymn and the homily, the curtain is drawn away, the Royal Gates are opened; the Deacon brings out the chalice with the Sacrament, stands on the Ambo, and calls out: "With the fear of God, and with faith draw near!" The faithful adore the Sacrament with a prostration, remembering Christ who rose from the dead and appeared to His disciples after His resurrection, and sing: "Blessed is He that cometh in the name of the Lord; the Lord is God, and hath manifested Himself unto us." Then the communicants approach the Ambo, make their profession of faith in the Sacrament of the Eucharist, and beseech the Lord that He may admit them to participate in His Last Supper and vouchsafe to let them receive His holy communion uncondemned.

Prayers before Communion.—"I believe, O Lord, and confess that Thou art in truth the Christ, the Son of the living God; Who camest into the world to save sinners, of whom I am the greatest. Also, I believe that this is Thy immaculate Body itself and this is Thy precious Blood itself. Wherefore, I beseech Thee, have mercy on me, and forgive my transgressions, voluntary and involuntary, committed in deed or in word, knowingly or unknowingly, and make me worthy, without condemnation, to partake of Thy most pure Mysteries, unto remission of sins, and unto life eternal."—"Receive me to-day, O Son of God, as a partaker of Thy mystic Supper; for I will not impart the mystery to Thine enemies, nor will I give Thee a kiss like Judas; but even as the Thief I confess unto Thee: Remember me, O Lord, in Thy Kingdom."—"Not unto my judgment, nor unto my condemnation be the participation in Thy holy Mysteries, O Lord, but unto the healing of my soul and body."

Then, after a prostration, the communicants, one by one, without crowding one another, and with hands reverently crossed on the breast, approach the chalice, receive the Body and Blood of Christ out of the spoon from the hands of the Priest, and very gently kiss the edge of the chalice, as it were the side of Christ Himself. As he gives the communion to each, the Priest says: "The servant (or handmaid) of God * * * partaketh of the precious and holy Body and Blood of our Lord and God, and Savior, Jesus Christ, unto remission of sins and unto life eternal." The communicant retires and makes a reverent obeisance, but not a prostration; for, having become mystically united to Christ, he is now a child of God, and the prostration is a sign of servitude. During the time that laymen receive communion, the choir repeatedly sings: "Receive the Body of Christ, taste of the immortal fount. Alleluia!" Having administered the Sacrament to all the communicants, the Priest carries the chalice to the altar and drops into it the portions taken out of the oblation-breads on behalf of the living and the dead.

The Blessing and the Last Appearance of the Holy Gifts Before the People.—This part of the Liturgy ends, like the preceding ones, with a blessing. Having placed the chalice upon the altar, the Priest steps out of the sanctuary, and standing on the Ambo, blesses the people, speaking this prayer: "Save Thy people, O Lord, and bless Thine inheritance." In answer to this, the choir sings an hymn which sets forth what mercies the people have received through Christ: "We have beheld the true Light; we have received the Heavenly Spirit; we have found the true faith; we worship the undivided Trinity, for it has saved us." While this hymn is being sung, the Priest censes the chalice, which holds the holy Gifts, and when it is ended, the Deacon carries the paten to the altar, and the Priest, taking up the chalice, faces the people and utters the concluding words of the Doxology: "Always—now, and ever, and unto the ages of ages." The faithful make an obeisance to the very ground, remembering the ascension of Christ to Heaven.

(D.) Conclusion of the Service.

Giving Thanks for Communion.—Having adored Christ, manifested for the last time in His holy Sacrament, the Christians sing the hymn of thanksgiving: "Let our mouth be filled with Thy praise O Lord, that we may sing Thy Glory, for that Thou hast vouchsafed to make us partake of Thy holy, divine, immortal and life-giving Mysteries; preserve us in Thy holiness, that all this day we may study Thy righteousness.

Alleluia." (*i.e. help us to preserve in ourselves the holiness which we have received through communion, that we may through this whole day study to live righteously, according to Thy word.*) The Deacon also gives thanks in the prayers of the Little Ectenia, which differs from the ordinary one in that instead of beginning with the words "Again and again," etc., it begins as follows: "Stand up! Having partaken of the divine, holy, undefiled, immortal, heavenly and life-giving dread Mysteries of Christ, let us worthily give thanks to the Lord."

Blessing for Going Forth Out of the Church;—Prayer Recited off the Ambo;—Distribution of Holy Bread;—and Dismissal.—After thanks have been given the Priest blesses the Christians who are to go forth out of the church, reminding them that they should go forth and live outside of it in the same peace with which they entered it. "In peace let us go forth," he says. To this the choir responds, speaking for all, "In the name of the Lord." Then the Priest, stepping down from the Ambo, and standing in the midst of the people, recites a prayer which is an epitome of the entire service. He prays that the Lord may save His people and bless His inheritance, the fullness of His Church (*i. e. the entire Christian community*), that He may preserve and sanctify those who love the splendor of His house, that He may not forsake us, who hope in Him, and that he may grant peace to the whole world; to His churches, to the priesthood, to the Emperor, to the army and to all men." The choir, speaking for all express the wish to go forth with the blessing of God: " Be the name of the Lord blessed now and forever," is sung thrice, after which Psalm 33 is read: " I will bless the Lord at all times."

During the reading of the Psalm the Priest distributes pieces of holy bread. These are the remnants of the oblation-loaf out of which a portion—the Lamb—has been cut in memory of Christ, and is called *Antidoron*, which means: " Substitute for the Gift." The Antidoron is distributed in order that those who have not received communion may also, at least in thought, share in the Sacrament of the Eucharist, that they may not feel left out of the community of the faithful, but in communion with them. The distribution of the Antidoron is a survival of the *agapes* or love-feasts which, among the early Christians, were made up of the remains of the offerings brought.

After the reading of the Psalm, and the distribution of the Antidoron, the priest blesses the people in the name of the Lord, saying "The blessing of the Lord be with you, by His grace and love toward men." The service ends with a prayerful wish that the Lord may have mercy on us at the intercession of the Mother of God, and of His Saints, and that He may give us length of days.

The communicants remain after the dismissal, to listen to more prayers of thanksgiving for communion.

NOTE 1. Days When the Liturgy of St. Basil the Great is Performed, and Wherein It Differs from That of St. John Chrysostom.—The Liturgy as ordered by St. Basil the Great, Archbishop of Cæsarea in Cappadocia, is performed only ten times in the year: on the Vigils of Christmas and Epiphany (if these vigils do not fall on a Saturday or Sunday, in which case the Liturgy of St. Basil the Great is performed on the feast-day itself, and that of St. John Chrysostom on the vigil); on the first of January, that being the day sacred to the memory of St. Basil; on the Sundays of Lent, with the exception of Palm Sunday; on Thursday and Saturday of the Holy Week.

The Liturgy of Basil the Great differs from that of John Chrysostom only in the following points: 1), the secret prayers, which the priest recites inaudibly while performing the sacrifice, are longer, and, therefore, the hymns which accompany the act, are sung to slower time;—2). the words of the institution of the Sacrament are given as follows: "He gave to His holy disciples and apostles and said: take and eat..." and "He gave to His holy disciples and apostles and said: take and drink...;"—3). in the place of the hymn "Meet it is," the hymn immediately following is sung: "In thee, thou full of grace, all creatures rejoice;"—and 4). in the dismissal prayer the name of Basil the Great is mentioned instead of John Chrysostom's.

NOTE 2. The Typica or Pro-Liturgy Service.—When, on days on which the church statutes prescribe that the Liturgy shall be celebrated, it is not possible to do so, either from the lack of a church or because the priest has failed to prepare himself for partaking of the Sacrament, the *Rite of the Typica* is substituted for the Liturgy. This service begins with the singing, immediately after the Great Ectenia, of the two Psalms, 102 ("Bless the Lord, O my Soul, and all that is within me bless His holy name"), and 145 ("Praise the Lord, O my Soul"), which, in the complete Liturgy, are used as Typical Antiphons. These Psalms are followed by the hymn "O only-begotten Son..." which contains the Christian doctrine of the Incarnation, and by the Beatitudes, with the penitent thief's prayer, "Remember me, O Lord, in Thy Kingdom," repeated between the verses. After the Beatitudes, the Epistle and the Gospel are read, the Triple Ectenia is recited, the Creed is chanted, followed by the Ectenia of Supplication, and, in conclusion, the Lord's Prayer and Dismissal.

SPECIAL FEATURES OF DIVINE SERVICE ON FEAST-DAYS AND IN FAST-TIME.

Immovable Feasts and Fasts.

THE UNIVERSAL FEAST OF THE EXALTATION OF THE PRECIOUS AND LIFE-GIVING CROSS OF THE LORD.

The Feast of the Exaltation of the Cross is celebrated on the 14th of September, in memory of two events: 1.) the finding by the Empress Helena, mother of the Emperor Constantine the Great, of the precious Cross on which Christ Savior was crucified, and 2.) the restoration of this same Cross from captivity with the Persians by the Greek Emperor Heraclius. The feast is named the *Exaltation*, because, when the Cross of Christ was found, it was elevated, "exalted," that all might see it, and *Universal* because the Christians, in their joy at the Cross's return from captivity, resolved that this event should be celebrated all over the world.

As the finding and exalting of the Cross of Christ was a triumph of the Christian faith, which the Emperors had declared the dominant religion of the Empire, the hymns for the day contain principally prayers for the pious Tsar and for the Christian people. This character is expressed in the Troparion for the day: "Save, O Lord, Thy people and bless Thine inheritance, granting our pious Emperor victories over his opponents and preserving the community by Thy Cross."

The chief peculiarity of the service is that, on the vigil of the feast, after Vespers, the Cross is brought out of the repository of sacred vessels, as though out of the depths of the earth, and is placed upon the altar. Then, at Matins, after the Great Doxology, to the slow singing of the Trisagion, it is brought out of the Sanctuary and placed on a specially decorated lectern, for public adoration. For this ceremony the Priest dons all the vestments of his order; he carries the Cross on his head, on a salver, coming through the northern door, in token that Christ, although invested with divine glory, came into the world in humiliation. All Christians, the celebrants first, then the laymen, approach the Cross, adore it with two prostrations, then kiss it and perform one more prostration. During all this time the choir sings the hymn: "Thy Cross we adore, O Master, and Thy holy Resurrection we glorify." In order that those absent from the church may, mentally at least, share in the adoration of the Cross, the church bells ring a carillon during the ceremony. The Cross remains on the lectern until the 21st of September, when, after the Liturgy and dismissal, it is solemnly taken up and carried into the Sanctuary through the Royal Gates.—The celebration of this feast is accompanied by severe fasting, in memory of the Passion of Christ, and as a token that the Christian should follow after Christ by the road of suffering, by mortifying his passions and carnal desires.

In great churches and in monasteries, the adoration is preceded by the ceremony of exalting the Cross. The Priest, having brought out the Cross, places it on the lectern, censes it, then, taking it up in his hands, stands with his face turned towards the East (towards the Sanctuary). During this time the Deacon recites an Ectenia consisting of five petitions; after each petition the "Lord have mercy on us" is chanted a hundred times. During the chanting of each hundred, the rite of exaltation is performed: the Priest elevates the Cross, first towards the East, then towards the West, South and North, then once more towards the East. At the beginning of each hundred, he makes the sign of the cross thrice in the direction in which he performs the exaltation; then, holding the Cross in his hands, he slowly bows his head nearly to the ground, then raises it as slowly; towards the end of the hundred he stands upright and blesses the people with the Cross thrice. After the exaltation takes place the adoration of the Cross.

THE NATIVITY OF OUR LORD GOD AND SAVIOR JESUS CHRIST.

Of all the twelve high feast-days, that of the Nativity of Christ (25th of December), is celebrated with particular solemnity. For the worthy celebration of it, Christians prepare by a fast of forty days, called the Fast of the Nativity (*Advent*), which lasts from the 15th of November to the 24th of December inclusively. It is popularly known also as "Philip's Fast" because it begins the day after that consecrated to the memory of the Apostle Philip (14th of November). Already from the day of the Virgin's Presentation in the Temple, hymns are sung in honor of the Nativity. Especially at Matins canticles from the Christmas Canon are sung: "Christ is born—glorify Him! Christ hath descended from Heaven—receive Him! Christ is on earth—be uplifted! Let all earth sing to the Lord, and ye, men, sing in gladness, for He is glorified." The two last Sundays before the Nativity are sacred to the memory of all the Old Testament Saints, who were saved by faith in the coming Savior. The first of these Sundays is called "the Sunday of the Ancient Fathers" and is consecrated to the memory of the holy Patriarchs, from Adam to Joseph, called the husband of Mary the Mother of God, and of the holy Prophets, from Samuel to John the Baptist; while the second is called "the Sunday of the Holy Fathers" and is consecrated to the memory of Christ's forefathers in the flesh.

The vigil of this feast is observed by keeping a strict fast. The Church prescribes that on this day boiled wheat be the only food used, or boiled rice with raisins and honey (*Kutyá*), irrespective of the day of the week. As to the services on this vigil, they differ according to the day of the week. If it falls on a Monday, Tuesday, Wednesday, Thursday or Friday, the so-called " Royal Hours " are read, which proclaim length of life to the Emperor, the Synod and the local bishop, then follow Vespers combined with the Liturgy of Basil the Great;* on Christmas Day itself the Liturgy of John Chrysostom is celebrated. If the vigil falls on a Saturday or on a Sunday, then: 1.) the Royal Hours are read on Friday, and on that Friday there is no Liturgy; 2.) on the vigil itself the Liturgy of Chrysostom is celebrated in the morning, then 3.) Vespers with Lessons from the Epistle and the Gospel after the Vesper Introit; 4.) on Christmas Day the Liturgy of Basil the Great is celebrated.

" Royal Hours " differ from the ordinary in the following points: 1.) of the three Psalms prescribed for each Hour only one is read; the other two are selected specially with reference to the events commemorated; 2.) at each Hour after the Troparia, the Parœmiæ, the Epistle and the Gospel, are read; and 3.) the offices of all the three Hours are combined into one. These Hours are called " Royal " because they are read only on the eve of the most important days of Christ's earthly life,—on the vigils of the Nativity and the Epiphany and on good Friday;—and also because in ancient times the Emperors used, on these days, to go in solemn procession to the principal church of the city.

The Liturgy or the Vespers service is followed by the "glorification of Christ:" a lighted candle is placed in the middle of the church, symbolizing the light of Christ, and the celebrants,

---

*Vespers and the Liturgy are combined in the following manner: after the Hours, Vespers begin with a blessing on the Reign of the Holy Trinity; then follows the Vesper Introit with the Gospel, after which the Prokimenon is sung and Parœmiæ are recited; these are followed by the Little Ectenia, which concludes with the Exclamation: " For Thou art holy, O our God; " then the Choir sings the Trisagion, the Epistle is read, and the Gospel; when the Liturgy proceeds as usual.

standing before it, sing the Troparion and the Kondakion of the feast. This ceremony is afterwards performed in the homes of Christians, desirous to bring the joy of Christmas into their own houses, their own families.

Troparion of the Nativity.—"Thy Nativity, O Christ our God, hath arisen on the world as the light of knowledge; for at it those that served the stars were taught by a Star to worship Thee, the Sun of Righteousness, and to know Thee, the Orient from on high. O Lord, glory to Thee."—*Kondakion.*—" The Virgin to-day bringeth forth the Pre-existing, *(Him Who was before all things);* and the earth offereth the Unapproachable One a cave. Angels with shepherds glorify Him; and the Magi journey with the Star; for our sakes He is born a little Child,—He, God that was before the ages."

The All-night Vigil before the Nativity consists of the Great Compline and Matins.—On the day of the Feast itself, after the Liturgy, is performed a Te-Deum of thanksgiving for " the deliverance from the invasion of the Gauls and twenty nations with them," in the year 1812. This service concludes with the proclamation of length of days to the Emperor, to his House and the Christ-loving army, and of " eternal remembrance " for the Emperor Alexander I.

The day following on the Nativity, the Most Holy Mother of God is celebrated, as the Person who was the instrument of the Incarnation of the Son of God. The Sunday following on the Nativity is called " the Sunday of the Divine Fathers," and is sacred to the memories of the Carpenter Joseph, Mary's betrothed husband, of King David, and of James, the brother of the Lord.* In honor of the great festival, fasting is dispensed with on the Wednesdays and Fridays between the day of the Nativity and the vigil of the Epiphany, whence these two weeks are called " unbroken."

THE BAPTISM OF OUR LORD GOD AND SAVIOR JESUS CHRIST.

The feast of the Baptism of our Lord, celebrated on the 6th day of January, is also called the *Theophany* or *Epiphany (Divine Manifestation, Manifestation from Above)*, because, at the bap-

---

*If this Sunday falls on the 1st of January, i. e., after the conclusion of the festivities of the Nativity, which is prescribed for the 31st of December, the service in honor of the Divine Fathers is performed on the 26th of December.

tism of Jesus Christ, the Trinity was present and manifested: the Son of God received baptism in the River Jordan; God the Father testified to His Son by a voice from Heaven; and the Holy Ghost, appearing in the form of a dove, confirmed the words of God the Father. In ancient times Catechumens used to receive the Sacrament of Baptism on the vigil of this day, whence it also received the name of "Feast of Illumination."

Troparion of the Feast:—" When Thou wast baptized in Jordan, O Lord, the worship of the Trinity was manifested: for the voice of the Father bare witness unto Thee, calling Thee His beloved Son, and the Spirit, in the form of a dove, confirmed the truth of the words. Thou that did appear, O Christ God, and illumine the world, glory to Thee."—*Kondakion of the Feast:*—" Thou didst appear to-day to the universe, and Thy light, O Lord, hath come upon us, who understandingly sing to Thee: Thou hast come, Thou hast appeared, O Light unapproachable."

The services on this day are the same as on the day of the Nativity of Christ. The vigil is a day of fast as strict as that of the Nativity; and on the day following the faithful congregate to celebrate " the worshipful and glorious Prophet and Precursor, John the Baptizer of Christ." *

The special feature of the service on the day of the Epiphany is " the consecration of the waters." In all churches it takes place on the vigil of the feast, after the Liturgy or Vespers. In some churches, it is repeated on the day of the Feast after the Liturgy, on rivers and lakes, whither the clergy go in procession, with cross and banners. The first consecration is retained as a reminder of the baptism which Catechumens used to receive on this day, and of the vows which we ourselves took at our own baptism. The second consecration takes place in memory of the Baptism of Our Lord; hence the procession is called " going to Jordan." The service of consecration consists in the chanting of Sticheræ, the reading of Parœmiæ, of Lessons

---

*If the vigil happens on any day from Monday to Friday inclusively, the service consists of the Royal Hours and the Liturgy of Basil the Great, comsostom is celebrated. If the vigil happens on a Saturday or Sunday, the Liturgy of Chrysostom is celebrated at the proper time, then Vespers, and on the day of the feast—the Liturgy of Basil the Great; and the Royal Hours are put back to Friday. The All-night's Vigil on the eve of the feast begins with Complines.

from the Epistle and the Gospels, prayers offered by the Priest for the consecration of the waters,* and in the thrice repeated immersion of the cross, to the chanting of the Troparion of the Feast. After the ceremony, the celebrants, as on the vigil of the Nativity, sing the Troparion and the Kondakion of the Feast in the middle of the church, standing before the lighted candle, then, carrying with them some of the consecrated water, go to the homes of their parishioners and sprinkle them with the water.

THE ANNUNCIATION.

The Feast of the Annunciation is celebrated on the 25th of March; on the day following the faithful congregate to celebrate the Archangel Gabriel, who brought the joyful tidings to the Vigin Mary. This Feast usually comes in Lent, sometimes on one of the first days of the Paschal week. But in spite of the Lenten time, it is celebrated so brightly as not to be darkened by the sad Lenten services of even the Holy Week. Nor is it lost in the radiancy of the Paschal Week. Christians thus express the fact that they look on the Annunciation as on the beginning of our salvation.

Troparion of the Feast:—" To-day is the crowning of our salvation and the manifestation of the Mystery which was from all eternity. The Son of God becometh the Son of the Virgin, and Gabriel announceth the good tidings of grace. Wherefore let us also cry with him to the Mother of God: Hail, full of grace, the Lord is with thee."

The special features of the services on the Feast of the Annunciation are determined by the day on which it falls. If on a Sunday or Monday in Lent, the All-night Vigil preceeding it begins with Vespers; if on any other day of the week—with Complines, because Vespers then combines with the Hours. At Matins on the day of this feast the Poly-elaion is sung, excepting

---

*In this prayer the Priest asks of the Lord that " He may impart unto these waters the blessing of Jordan, so that all who take from it and partake of it may do so unto the cleansing of body and soul, unto healing from passions, unto the sanctification of their homes and unto every kind of benefit,"—and that " He may sanctify the water and grant unto all who touch it or anoint themselves therewith sanctification, health, purification and benediction."

when the Annunciation falls on the first day of Easter. In that case the Poly-elaion is omitted, the Canon of the Feast is sung together with the Paschal Canon, and the Gospel of the Annunciation is read after the sixth Ode of the Canon. The combination of the two feasts is called *Kyriopascha, i. e.* "the Lord's Pascha."—The Hours are the same for the Annunciation as for the day on which the feast falls: on Saturdays and Sundays, the ordinary Hours, on other days—the Lenten Hours, on Good Friday the Royal Hours and through the Paschal Week— the Paschal Hours. On the days on which the Lenten or the Royal Hours are prescribed, the Liturgy is celebrated after Vespers in combination with this service. If the Annunciation falls on any Sunday of Lent except Palm Sunday, or on Thursday or Saturday of the Holy Week, the Liturgy of Basil the Great is given, on all other days that of John Chrysostom.

The Day of the Holy and Most Glorious Apostles Peter and Paul.

The feast of the Apostles Peter and Paul is celebrated on the 29th of June. On the following day the faithful congregate to celebrate the Twelve Apostles. The special feature of this feast is the fast which precedes it, beginning one week after Pentecost and ending on the vigil of St. Peter's day. This fast the Church designates as "the Apostles'," but the people call it simply "Peter's Fast." It is observed in memory of the fact that the Apostles fasted before they went forth to preach the Gospel.

The Transfiguration of Our Lord and Savior Jesus Christ.

The Transfiguration of our Lord is celebrated on the 6th of August. It is the rule to bring to the churches on this day, for consecration, the first-fruits of fruit-bearing trees. In the East they bring grapes; we in Russia bring apples.*

---

*In the prayer for the consecration of the fruit of the vine the priest asks that the Lord may bless them, that they may be to us unto rejoicing, and that He may accept of a gift of these fruits unto the cleansing of our sins. When consecrating other first-fruit (such as apples), he prays that the Lord may receive our gift into His eternal treasury and grant us an abundance of worldly goods.

The substance of this feast's hymns is expressed in the Troparion for the day: "Upon the Mountain Thou wert transfigured, O Christ our God, showing Thy Glory to Thy disciples as much as they could bear. May Thy eternal Light shine forth for us also, through the prayers of the Mother of God. O, Giver of light, glory to Thee."

The Assumption[*] of the Mother of God.

For the worthy celebration of the Feast of the Assumption we prepare by a fast beginning on the 1st of August and lasting until the day of the Feast—15th of August. The Church calls it "Assumption Fast," but the people also give it the name of "Lady's Fast," because it is observed in honor of Our Lady the Queen of Heaven. At Matins on Assumption Day a *Acathistos* is read. This name is given to a collection of 24 short hymns in honor of the event or person commemorated on a certain day. It is not allowed to sit during the singing of these hymns, whence the Greek name of the collection: *Akathistos* means "not sitting."

The substance of the Assumption hymns is expressed in the Troparion for the day: "In child-birth thou didst retain thy virginity; in thy Repose thou didst not forsake the world, O Mother of God. Thou hast passed away into life, being the Mother of Life, and by thine intercessions thou dost deliver our souls from death."

. .

The Decollation (Beheading) of the Honorable Glorious Prophet and Precursor, John the Baptist.

This event is commemorated on the 29th of August. As men, on this day, once forgot righteousness and conscience in the midst of feasting, it is ordered that it should be a day of fasting, as a reminder to us to look well after the purity of our souls in the midst of pleasures and amusements. One of the features of this feast is the commemoration of the soldiers who died in battle for their faith and country; it takes place after the Liturgy.

---

[*] The Slavic word means literally "the going to sleep" or "to repose."

The Bringing Forth of the Holy and Life-giving Cross.

On this day—the 1st of August—two feasts are combined: 1) the bringing forth of the holy and life-giving Cross, and 2) the celebration of the All-merciful Savior, Christ God and the Holy Virgin Mary, His Mother. This is one of the lesser feasts. In Constantinople, on the 1st of August, the Life-giving Cross used to be brought forth from the palace and carried to the church of St. Sophia, and the ceremony of consecrating the waters was performed on this occasion. After this, for fifteen days, the Cross was carried through the streets of the city, with prayers for the preservation of the people from mortal epidemics and pestilence, because at this time of the year there usually was much sickness among the people; then the Cross was carried back into the palace. In 1164 the second celebration was added, in memory of two victories gained on this day: one by the Greek Emperor Manuel over the Saracens, and one by the Russian Prince Andreas Bogoliubsky over the Bulgars.

The special feature of the feast is the bringing forth of the Cross for adoration. This is done as on the day of the Exaltation. Only the ceremony of elevation itself is nowhere performed. After the Liturgy, and sometimes after Matins processions go to lakes, ponds, and rivers, where the lesser consecration of the waters takes place. The lesser consecration differs from the great consecration, on the day of the Epiphany, in that the prayer recited by the priest is shorter,* and at the immersion of the cross the verse, " Save Thy people, O Lord," is sung, and not, " To Thee, O Lord, that art baptized in Jordan."

Movable Feasts and Fasts.

All the movable days of worship are connected with the Greatest Christian feast, Easter, "the Day of the Pascha." Some of them are a preparation for the worthy celebration of this feast, others continue the festivities, making us sensible of its fruits.

---

*In this prayer the priest asks that, through partaking of this water, and besprinkling therewith, the Lord may send down upon us His benediction, " which washeth away the pollution of the passions."

The preparation for the feast consists of two fasts, that of the Great Quadragesima, beginning on the Monday of the first week and ending with the Friday of the sixth,—and the fast of the Holy Week. These two fasts are united by two days of which one, Saturday, is sacred to the memory of the Resurrection of Lazarus, and the other, Sunday, to that of Christ's entrance into Jerusalem. Both fasts together are called "the Great Fast," or "Lent." Over and above these weeks, three weeks are set apart as a preparation for Lent. Thus the whole time of preparation for the Paschal Feast comprises ten weeks.

The Paschal Feast lasts seven days. But the festivities do not end with these. The hymns in honor of the Resurrection are sung up to the day of the Ascension; then for two more Sundays, the Church speaks of the fruits which the Resurrection bore for our good; one is sacred to the memory of the Descent of the Holy Ghost upon the Apostles, and the other commemorates all the Saints who have obtained the Kingdom of Heaven through faith in the Lord crucified and risen from the dead.

The Weeks of Preparation for Lent.

Lent is a time of penance, and as penance requires a sense of one's unworthiness, hope in the mercy of the Lord, fear of judgment and a readiness to forgive others, all these feelings must be aroused in us before the beginning of Lent.

Three sennights before Lent, on Sunday, the parable of the Publican and the Pharisee is read, and in the Matin hymns the meaning of it is explained, which is a lesson of humility. This Sunday is called, "the Sunday of the Publican and Pharisee," and from it until the Sunday of the fifth week of Lent, after the hymn "Having seen the resurrection of Christ"... penitential Troparia are sung, inculcating humility. Besides this, that we may be taught still more clearly not to take pride in and boast of fulfilling the law, as the Pharisee of the parable boasted of keeping the fasts, the fast of the Wednesday and Friday is remitted for the following week.

Penitential Troparia:—" Open to me the door of repentance, O Life-giver, for my spirit doth long from early morning for Thy holy temple, bearing its corporal temple all defiled; but do Thou, that art bountiful, purify me by Thy loving mercy."—" Direct me to the path of salvation, O Mother of God, for I have polluted my soul with the vileness of sin, and have lived all my days in slothfulness; but do thou, by thine intercessions, deliver me from all impurity."—" Reflecting on the many iniquities committed by me, accursed that I am, I tremble at the fearful day of Judgment; but, trusting in the mercy of Thy lovingkindness, even as David, I cry unto Thee ' Have mercy on me, O God, by Thy great mercifulness.' "

On the following Sunday, during the Liturgy, the parable of the Prodigal Son is read, which teaches us, having repented of our sins, not to despair of our salvation, but to trust in the mercy of the Lord, our Heavenly Father. This Sunday is called, " the Sunday of the Prodigal Son." The essence of the hymns of the day is expressed in the Psalm: " By the rivers of Babylon, there we sat down and wept when we remembered Zion." This Psalm is sung at Matins after the Poly-elaion Psalms.

On the Sunday following that of the Prodigal Son, the Lesson from the Gospel is that on the Day of Judgment, that we, in trusting to God's mercy, may not forget His justice and may not lapse into carelessness. This Sunday is called, " the Sunday of Meat Fare," because with it ends the eating of meat. On the day before—Saturday—the Church commemorates, *i. e.* prays for, all our deceased forefathers, fathers and brethren, for whom the time of repentance is past, and who can obtain the mercy of God only through the prayers of the living. The Matin service on this Saturday consists mostly of prayers for the rest of their souls.

This Sunday is followed by the " Butter-and-Cheese Week " (Carnival Week), which is the vestibule to Lent. It has received this name because, all through it, the use of butter, cheese and eggs is allowed. In all the hymns of this week the Fall of Adam is referred to, and it is shown that it was caused by intemperance. On Wednesday and Friday of this week there is no Liturgy, but only a Lenten service. The last day of the week, Sunday, is called, " the Sunday of Cheese Fare," because with it ends the eating of butter, cheese and eggs. The Gospel Lesson, at the Liturgy of the day, commands us to forgive one another's sins. This is why Christians on this day ask one another's forgiveness for mutual offenses, and make efforts to become mutually reconciled. Hence the day is called "the Day of Forgiveness."

Peculiarities of Lenten Services.

The general feature of Lenten services is their increased duration with lessened splendor; in particular a limited number of joyful and triumphal hymns, subdued light, less frequent drawing away of the curtain and opening of the Royal Gates. Most of the services are performed with the Royal Gates closed and consist of the reading of Psalms and penitential prayers, listened to kneeling and with frequent prostrations. At every service the penitential prayer of Ephrem the Syrian is recited with prostrations: " O Lord and Master of my life ! the spirit of vanity, of idleness, of domination, of idle speech, give me not. But the spirit of chastity, of humility, of patience, of love, do Thou grant to me, Thy servant. Yea, O Lord and King, grant me that I may perceive my transgressions and not condemn my brother, for Thou art blessed unto the ages of ages. Amen." At Matins, every day except Saturday and Sunday, " Alleluia " is sung instead of " God is the Lord and hath appeared unto us."

The Liturgy being a joyful, triumphal service, it is celebrated during Lent only on Saturdays and Sundays; on the other days only the Typica, or Pro-Liturgy service is performed. Yet, in order that Christians may not be deprived for long of the privilege of partaking of the Sacrament of the Eucharist, it is permitted to give communion on certain days at Vespers, using *Pre-sanctified Gifts.* Such a Vesper service at which the faithful may receive communion, is called, " the Liturgy of the Pre-sanctified," also the Liturgy of Gregory the Great, because the ritual of it was written down by the Roman Patriarch, Saint Gregory the Great.

There is a special combination of services prescribed for Lent. The evening service consists of Complines; the morning service of Matins and the First Hour; the noon service of the Third, Sixth and Ninth Hours, of the Pro-Liturgy service, and of Vespers, combined on certain days with the Liturgy of the Presanctified.

The Lenten Hours.—The peculiarity of the offices of the Hours in Lent, consists in this, that at every Hour: 1) After the Three Psalms the Kathisma is read; 2) in the place of the Troparia for the day, special Troparia are read, indicating the events commemorated in the service for the given Hour; 3) before the concluding prayer of the Hour, the penitential prayer of the Hour is recited, with prostrations. At the Sixth Hour, over and above all the above mentioned, a Parœmia is read.

Troparion of the First Hour: "From the morning hear my voice, O my King and Lord."—*Of the Third Hour:*—"O Lord, that didst send down Thy most Holy Spirit at the third hour upon Thine Apostles, do not, O Merciful One, withdraw it from us, but regenerate us that pray unto Thee."— *Of the Sixth Hour:*—"Thou that, at the sixth hour of the sixth day, didst nail to the cross the daring sin of Adam committed in Paradise, O Christ God, do Thou tear up the written bond of our debt also, and save us."—*Of the Ninth Hour:*—"Thou that, at the ninth hour, didst taste of death in the flesh for our sakes, O Christ God, do Thou mortify the rebellion of our flesh and save us."

The Liturgy of the Pre-Sanctified.—The Liturgy of the Presanctified is celebrated on those days of Lent when the contrition proper to the season does not allow of the triumphal gladness conveyed by the full Liturgy, yet the memories of the day demand the comfort of the Communion Sacrament. Such days are the Wednesdays and Fridays in Lent, the first three days of Holy Week, and all the days on which falls the feast of some Saint, in whose honor the Poly-elaion is prescribed. At this Liturgy the gifts are not consecrated, but the faithful who receive communion partake of the Gifts which have been consecrated at the preceding Liturgy of Basil the Great or of John Chrysostom, and preserved in an ark on the altar. Therefore, the Liturgy of the Pre-sanctified consists only in the bringing of the Holy Gifts, the preparation for communion, the act of communion, and the thanksgiving for communion. This service is combined with that of Vespers only, as Catechumens may be present at Vespers, but only the faithful may witness the Liturgy; therefore, at the end of the Vesper service, before the Holy Gifts are transferred to the altar, the Catechumens are bid to depart.

Until the Vesper Introit the service proceeds as usual, with the only difference that it begins with the benediction of the Kingdom of the Holy Trinity, as when the complete Liturgy is celebrated: "Blessed is the Kingdom of the Father, and of the Son, and of the Holy Ghost." The initiatory exclamation of the Priest is followed by the Prefatory Psalm, the Great Ectenia, the Kathisma, divided into three sections or Antiphons by the Little Ectenia, recited twice,—the Psalm, "O Lord, I have cried," with Sticheræ, and the hymn, "O tranquil Light." Before this latter hymn is sung the Royal Gates are opened and the Priest enters with the censer, or—if it be a day on which a Lesson from the Gospels is to be read—with the Testament. After the Introit the Prokimenon is sung, the Royal Gates are closed, and two Parœmiæ for the day are read; on feast-days the Parœmia of the feast is added. After the first Parœmia the Royal Gates are again opened and the Prokimenon of the first Parœmia is sung. Then the Priest takes in his hands a censer and a lighted candle, exclaims: "Wisdom! Stand up!" to arouse the attention of the worshippers, and makes the sign of the cross over them with the censer and the candle, with the words: "the Light of Christ illumineth all," in token that the Old Testament Saints, whose words are read in the Parœmiæ, were also illumined by the same light as the New Testament man, that they lived and were saved by faith in the coming Christ as we are saved by faith in Christ come. At this moment the faithful adore Christ, the Light of Truth, with a prostration. This ceremony is a survival of the ancient custom of making the sign of the cross with a candle during Lent over the Catechumens who were preparing for baptism before Easter; it was done in anticipation of the illumination which the Catechumens were to receive through this Sacrament. After the ceremony, the Royal Gates are closed once more, and the second Parœmia is read.

After the Parœmiæ, in order to arouse more strongly the feeling of penitence, the worshippers listen kneeling to the verses of the Psalm which were sung before the Introit, and which now are sung again with deep contrition: "Let my prayer be set forth as incense before Thee; the lifting up of my hands as the evening sacrifice.—Lord, I have called unto Thee, hear me; give ear unto me when I call unto Thee.—Set a watch, O Lord, before my mouth; keep the door of my lips.—Incline not my heart to words of guile, to shift from me the guilt of my sins."— Then the worshippers express their repentance by repeating the prayer of Ephrem the Syrian, with three prostrations. Here follow Lessons from the Gospels and the Epistle, if such are prescribed; if they are not, the Triple Ectenia is recited. The general prayer of the Vesper service end with the Ectenia for the Catechumens and with the latter departing from the church. The faithful remain, and the special prayers of the Liturgy begin.

The Liturgy begins with two Little Ecteniæ, each ending with the exclamation, "Wisdom!" after which the Cherubic Hymn is sung during the transfer of the Holy Gifts: "Now the hosts of Heaven invisibly minister with us; for lo! the King of Glory entereth; lo! the mystic sacrifice consummated (*i. e. already sanctified,*) is borne on high. With faith and love let us draw near, that we may become partakers of Life eternal. Alleluia!" At the words, "borne on high" the singing is suspended; the Priest enters through the northern door, bearing on his head the paten, on which repose the Pre-sanctified Gifts, and in his hand the chalice with the wine, and enters the Sanctuary through the Royal Gates, without speaking. The faithful adore with a prostration Christ, Who passed before them in the Sacrament. After the Priest has entered the Sanctuary, the Royal Gates are closed, the curtain is drawn to and the choir takes up and ends the Cherubic Hymn.

After the transfer of the Holy Gifts the faithful prepare for communion; the Triple Ectenia is recited, the Lord's Prayer is chanted, the Priest offers " Peace to all," proclaims "The Presanctified Holy to the holy!" to which the faithful respond by singing, " One is holy, One is the Lord," then the Communion Hymn is sung: " Taste and see, for the Lord is good. Alleluia!"

The communion of the celebrants and the laymen, the giving of thanks, and the dismissal take place as usual. Only, instead of " Blessed is He Who cometh in the name of the Lord," the choir sing the hymn: " I will bless God at all times; His praise is on my lips. Taste of the Cup of Life and see how good the Lord is"; and when the Priest descends from the Ambo, he reads a prayer in which he asks that the Lord may " cause us to worthily perform the good work, to accomplish the course of Lent, to remain victorious over sin and live, without incurring judgment, to adore the holy Resurrection."

SPECIAL FEATURES OF THE SERVICES IN EACH WEEK OF THE QUADRAGESIMA.

Each of the successive weeks of the Quadragesima presents some special feature in the services. At the Great Compline, the first four days of the first week, the penitential Canon composed by Andreas of Crete is read. The Troparia of this Canon call our attention to the virtues and transgressions of the men who are spoken of in Holy Scripture, and urge us to imitate the former and shun the example of the latter. The burden of the Canon is the prayer, " Have mercy on me, Lord, have mercy on me." On the Wednesday and Thursday, to this Canon is added that of Mary the Egyptian, who was at first a great sinner, then a great penitent and ascete. This latter was also composed by Andreas of Crete, and teaches us not to despair of our salvation, but to labor at our self-improvement, while trusting in the help of God. This Compline office is also called *Ephymnion*—a Greek word, which means, " the burden or refrain of a song."

On the Saturday of the first week there is a celebration in honor of St. Theodore Tyro, Martyr. It begins already on Friday at Vespers, when, after the Liturgy of the Pre-sanctified, a prayer is said for the blessing of the wheat food (*Kolívo, Kutyá* —boiled wheat with honey.) This celebration commemorates the following occasion. The Greek Emperor Julian, apostate from the faith, wishing to pollute the Christians by the use of food forbidden by the Church, secretly ordered that every article of food placed for sale on the markets, in the first week of Lent, should be sprinkled with the blood of animals sacrificed to the idols. But St. Theodore appeared to the Bishop of the city in a vision, made known to him Julian's secret order, and advised that the Christians should buy no eatables in the markets during the whole week, but live on boiled wheat with honey.

On the first Sunday of Lent the "Triumph of Orthodoxy" is celebrated, in memory of the restoration of the adoration of holy ikons under the Empress Theodora (862 A. D.). The special feature of the day's service consists in this, that, in Cathedral churches, before the Liturgy and after the Hours, or just before the end of the Liturgy, the celebrants come into the middle of the church, bearing ikons of the Savior and of the Mother of God, and having placed them on lecterns, perform before them a special service with singing, consisting chiefly in petitions that the Lord may establish Christians in the true belief and incline apostates and heretics to return to the right path. At the end of the service, the Deacon, in a loud voice, recites the Creed, to impress on Orthodox Christians the doctrine which they are to hold; after which he enumerates all the false doctrines, pronounces *anathema* against all those who receive them,—i. e. separation from the Church or exclusion from the community of Orthodox Christians—and "eternal remembrance" for the defenders of the faith. The service concludes with the proclamation of "length of days" to the reigning House, to the Orthodox Patriarchs, to the Clergy, and to all Orthodox Christians, and with the petition that the Lord may keep them firm in the true faith, and convert and bring to the knowledge of eternal truth the traducers and blasphemers of the Orthodox Faith and Church and those who rebel against them. Then the hymn, "Thee, O God, we praise," is sung, during which the worshippers express their reverence for ikons by adorations and kisses.

On the third Sunday of Lent, at Matins, after the Great Doxology, the Cross is brought out into the middle of the church as on the day of the Exaltation, for adoration, to the singing of the hymn, "Thy Cross we adore, O Master, and Thy Resurrection we glorify." The Cross remains in the church all through the week, but the adoration takes place only on Monday and Wednesday, at the office of the First Hour, and on Friday after the service of the Hours, when the Cross is taken back into the Sanctuary. From this ceremony the third Sunday and the week following after it (fourth of Lent), have the name of "Week of the Adoration of the Cross."

On Thursday of the fifth week (following on the fourth Sunday), at Matins, the entire penitential Canon of Andreas of Crete is read together with the Canon in honor of Mary the Egyptian. On this day the Liturgy of the Pre-sanctified is celebrated.

On Saturday of the fifth week, at Matins, an Akathistos in honor of the Virgin is read, in remembrance of the deliverance, on this day, of Constantinople from the invading Persians and Avars in the seventh century through the intercession of the Virgin, whose ikon was carried around the walls of the city.

Special Features of the Services on the Sabbath of Lazarus and Palm Sunday.

These two days are the preliminary to the fast of the Holy Week. The Saturday commemorates the raising of Lazarus from the dead, and is called, "the Resurrection of Lazarus."

Because this event manifested the divine might of Christ, and prepared His solemn entrance into Jerustlem, and, on the other hand, gave the assurance that all the dead should rise, therefore, at Matins are sung the Sunday Troparia "The angel hosts were amazed," and the hymn "Having beheld the Resurrection of Christ," while the prayers for the souls of the dead, usually sung on Saturdays, are omitted.

The Sunday following on this Saturday commemorates the solemn entrance of Christ into Jerusalem, and is one of the Twelve Feasts.

At Matins, after the reading from the Gospels, the consecration of the palms takes place; (in our country budding willow branches are substituted for the palm branches). All through the singing of the Canon the worshippers hold in their hands these branches and lighted candles. From this ceremony the day has the name of Palm Sunday.

The essence of the hymns of this day and the meaning of the ceremony of consecrating the palms are expressed in the Troparion of the Feast: "Before Thy passion, O Christ God, Thou didst raise Lazarus from the dead, giving us assurance of a common resurrection. Therefore we also, like unto children bearing the banner of victory, cry unto Thee, the Vanquisher of Death, 'Hosanna in the highest, blessed He that cometh in the name of the Lord.'"

Special Features of the Services on the First Three Days of Passion Week.

The Monday, Tuesday and Wednesday of Passion (Holy) Week commemorate the last communings of Jesus with the people and His disciples. These communings make up the substance of nearly all the hymns of these days.* At Matins, after the Alleluia, instead of "God is the Lord" is sung the Troparion: "Behold the Bridegroom cometh in the middle of the night, and blessed is that servant whom He shall find watching; but unworthy is he whom he shall find careless. Beware, then, my soul, lest thou be weighed down by sleep, lest thou be given over to death, and shut out from the Kingdom, but spring up crying, 'Holy, holy, holy art Thou, O God; for the sake of the Mother of God, have mercy on us.'" After the Canon is

---

* Some of the hymns of the Monday bring before us Joseph, sold by his brothers, as the prototype of Christ; and in the barren fig-tree, cursed by the Lord Jesus, we are shown the Jews who betrayed and put him to death. The hymns of the Tuesday bid us prepare to meet the Heavenly Bridegroom, who receiveth into His chamber only such as have bridal garments woven of virtues—those who meet Him with the lighted lamp of faith and good deeds, and have not hidden but increased the talents given them by God. The hymns of the Wednesday recall the supper at Simon's, at which the sinning woman anointed Christ's feet with myrrh.

sung the hymn: "Thine halls I behold, O my Savior, all adorned, and I have no garments that I may enter therein; irradiate the vestment of my soul, O Giver of Light, and save me." On these three days the Liturgy of the Pre-sanctified is celebrated, with Lessons from the Gospels. The Gospel is read also at Matins. And besides all this, in order to bring before us more vividly and fully the entire life of Christ, the Church prescribes to read all the four Gospels through on these days, at the Offices of the Hours. From the importance of the events commemorated, all the days of the Passion Week are called "holy" and "great."

SPECIAL FEATURES OF THE SERVICE ON HOLY THURSDAY.

The service of Holy Thursday commemorates the washing of the disciples' feet, the Last Supper, Christ's praying in the garden of Gethsemane and His betrayal by Judas. The special features of the day are the following: A Parœmia is read at the First Hour; the Liturgy of Basil the Great is celebrated in combination with Vespers; at the Liturgy, instead of the Cherubic Hymn, the Communion Prayer, the verse during the act of communion, and the hymn, "Let your lips be filled with praise," the choir sings: "Receive me this day, O Son of God, as partaker in Thy Last Supper."

In Cathedral churches, after the prayer which the Priest descends from the Ambo to recite, the ceremony of the washing of the feet is performed. The Bishop comes forth and steps on an Ambo placed in the middle of the church (*the robing platform*); there he takes his seat in an armchair before a lectern on which lies a Testament. Then the Deacon leads forth from the Sanctuary twelve priests, two by two, and they take seats on both sides of the Bishop in two rows, from the platform to the Royal Gates. During this time the choir sings Sticheræ in which the washing of the disciples' feet by the Lord at the Last Supper is referred to. When all the twelve priests, representing the disciples at the Supper, are in their places, the Deacon recites the Great Ectenia, adding a petition that the Lord, "may bless this washing, that it may be for the cleaning of the pollution of our transgressions." During the recital of the Ectenia the Bishop and the priests remain seated; when it is concluded the Bishop alone rises, offers up a prayer, that "the Lord may deign to let the contact of this water wash us of all spiritual impurity and to preserve us from the spiritual serpent, which striveth to bite our heel," and sits down again. Then, all the celebrants remaining seated, begins the reading of the Gospel Lesson, telling how Christ, at the Last Supper, washed His disciples' feet. As the Deacon utters the words " He riseth from supper," the Bishop rises; at the words " and laid aside His garments," he lays aside his episcopal vestments: the Panagia, the pectoral cross, the Omophorion, the Thigh-shield and the Saccos. During the disrobing the Deacon keeps repeating the words "and laid aside His garments." The Deacon reads on: "and took a towel and girded Himself;" the Bishop then girds himself with a towel. The Deacon reads, " After that He poureth water into a basin "—and the Bishop pours water from an ewer into a basin. When the Deacon reads " and began to wash the disciples' feet, and to wipe them with the towel wherewith He was girded," the Bishop washes the feet of the twelve priests, beginning with him who sits first on the left hand side, and ending with him who sits first on the right hand side. The order of the washing is as follows: the Bishop pours water thrice from his hand on each priest's foot, wipes it with the towel and kisses the priest's hand; and he whose foot has been washed, kisses the Bishop's mitre and hand. While the feet of eleven of the priests are washed, the Deacon keeps repeating the words "and began to wash the disciples' feet and to wipe them with the towel wherewith He was girded." As the Deacon reads " Then cometh He to Simon Peter: and Peter said unto him," the Bishop approaches the priest who sits first on the right hand side; the priest rises from his seat and says in the words of the Gospel: " Lord, dost Thou wash my feet?" The Bishop replies, also in the words of the Gospel: " What I do, thou knowest not now, but thou shalt know hereafter." The priest continues to speak in the words of the Gospel: "Thou shalt never wash my feet." The Bishop replies: "If I wash thee not, thou hast no part with me." Then the priest says " Lord, not my feet only, but my hands and my head," pointing to his hands and head, and resumes his seat. The Bishop replies in the words of the Gospel: " He that is washed needeth not but to wash his feet, but is clean every whit: and ye are clean, but not all "—and washes the priest's foot, after which he returns to his place on the platform and takes off the towel, and the Deacon reads the end of the Gospel Lesson: " For He knew who should betray Him; therefore said He ' Ye are not all clean.' " The choir now sing " Glory to Thee, our God, glory to Thee"; then the Deacon again invites those present to listen attentively to the Gospel, and continues reading: "After He had washed their feet and had taken His garments." The words "and had taken His garments" are repeated many times, while the Bishop resumes his vestments. As the Deacon reads the words " and was set down again," the Bishop sits down and all the priests rise to their feet. Then the Bishop himself reads the end of the Gospel Lesson: "I have given you an example, that ye should do as I have done to you." The Bishop then rises and offers a prayer, that "the Lord may wash away all impurity from our souls, and that we, having washed away the dust of transgressions that did cling to our souls, may wipe one another with the towel of love and gain the strength to please God." Then the Bishop enters the Sanctuary and goes on with the Liturgy.

At the Church of the Assumption in Moscow and in the Laura of the Catacombs at Kief (*Kievo-Petcherskaya Lavra*) there takes place on Holy Thursday the consecration of the myrrh or chrism which is used in all the churches in Russia for the Sacraments of Confirmation, at the consecration of churches and Antiminses, and at the coronation of a Tsar. The preparation of the ingredients begins from the week of the Adoration of the Cross. The ingredients are: olive oil, wine, sweet-smelling oils, various kinds of incense and herbs (thirty in all). The oil is emblematic of mercy, the wine of Christ's Blood, the perfumes symbolize the manifold gifts of the Holy Ghost. From Monday of the Holy Week, the mixture of oil and wine simmers in kettles to the continuous reading of the Gospels. On Wednesday the aromatic ingredients are added and the myrrh is poured out of the kettles into vessels. On Thursday, before the Liturgy, the Bishop and priests, in full canonicals, transfer the vessels containing the new myrrh and a vessel containing last year's myrrh to the church, and place them on and around the Table of Oblations. At the great procession with the Holy Gifts, the vessels with the myrrh are also transferred from the Table of Oblations to the altar. The vessel with last year's myrrh is placed upon the altar; the vessels with the new myrrh are disposed around it. After the exclamation " And may the mercies of the Lord, our God and Savior, Jesus Christ, abide with you all!" the consecration of the myrrh takes place. The Bishop blesses each vessel thrice with the words " In the name of the Father and of the Son and of the Holy Ghost," then prays that the Lord " may send down upon the myrrh the grace of the Holy Ghost, and make it a spiritual anointment, a repository of life, a sanctification of bodies and souls, an oil of gladness." After the Ectenia of Supplication and commemoration of all the Saints, the myrrh is taken into the repository of sacred vessels. There, into each vessel of new myrrh are poured a few drops of the old myrrh, and the vessel which holds the latter is replenished with new myrrh. This is done in token of the uninterrupted connection of the Russian Church with the Greek, from which she received the grace of priesthood in the person of her first bishop and also received the first consecrated myrrh.

Special Features of the Services on Good Friday.

The services on Good Friday commemorate the Passion of Christ. Matins begin at the second hour of night (the eighth hour p. m. on Thursday, as we count time). There is no Kathisma, but after the Great Ectenia and the " Alleluia," the twelve Gospel Lessons are read which narrate the Passion of

Christ, beginning with His last discourse with His disciples at the Last Supper, and ending with His entombing in the garden of Joseph of Arimathæa. Between the Lessons anthems are sung, in which Judas' treason and the Jews' malice are denounced, then the Triodion and Sticheræ. The service ends with the Ecteniæ. During the reading of the Gospel Lessons, the faithful stand with lighted candles in their hands. This service is called " the succession of the holy and saving passions of Our Lord Jesus Christ "—familiarly " the Passions." There is no Liturgy on Good Friday. The Royal Hours are read, in which the Psalms, the Troparia, the Parœmiæ, the Epistle and Gospel Lessons all have reference to Christ's Passion. Vespers begin at the tenth hour of day, (the third hour p. m.) At this service, after the Introit, are read three Parœmiæ, and Lessons from the Epistle and the Gospels. (The Gospel Lesson is composed of the narratives of the three Evangelists—Matthew, Luke and John, of the Passion of Christ, from the conference of the Jews to the Savior's death.) After the Sticheræ the "Sepulchre" is brought out of the Sanctuary and placed in the middle of the church. This is a painting, generally on canvas, representing Christ entombed, in memory of the taking down from the cross of the body of Christ. This ceremony takes place to the singing of the Troparion " The noble Joseph, having taken Thy immaculate Body from the tree, and wrapped it in a clean linen cloth with spices, laid it and covered it in a new grave." The canvas is laid out on a table, and all present adore it and kiss the wounds of Christ, in the side, the hands and the feet. If the Feast of the Annunciation happens on this day, Vespers take place earlier, combined with the Liturgy of John Chrysostom, and the " Sepulchre " is brought out at the Little Compline.

SPECIAL FEATURES OF THE SERVICES ON HOLY SATURDAY.

On Holy Saturday, after " God is the Lord " and the Troparia, the 118th Psalm is sung: " Blessed are the undefiled in the way, who walk in the law of the Lord," verse by verse. The verses of the Psalm are divided by refrains which are called " praises " because they contain a glorification of the dead and entombed Lord. All present during this time hold lighted candles in their hands. The Psalm is followed by the Sunday Troparia and Canon. During the Canon, the celebrants don the full sacerdotal vestments and, after the Great Doxology, take up the "Sepulchre," to the singing of the funeral Trisagion, and carry it in procession, either outside around the church or inside around the Sanctuary and church, in memory of the entombing of the Lord. When it is restored to its place in the middle of the church, the Ecteniæ are recited, the Parœmiæ are read, as well as the Epistle and Gospel; then follows the adoration before the "Sepulchre."

The Liturgy is celebrated on this day after the rite of Basil the Great, and is combined with Vespers. As the latter service has reference to the next day—Sunday, the hymns commemorating the entombing of Christ alternate during the Liturgy with those belonging to the Sunday service. After the evening Introit,—which, on this day, takes place with the Testament, fifteen Parœmiæ are read, containing prophecies and prototypes of salvation through the passion and resurrection of Christ. The Lesson from the Epistle tells us that, through Baptism, we are entombed together with Christ. Before the Gospel Lesson, the choir, instead of "Alleluia," sings the Prokimenon "Rise, O God, and judge the earth, for Thine is the inheritance in all nations." While this Prokimenon is sung, the celebrants change their vestments and the decorations of the church are changed. The Gospel Lesson tells of Christ rising from the dead. Instead of "Meet it is" the Irmos of the 9th Ode of the Matin Canon is sung and instead of the Cherubic Hymn the hymn: "Let all human flesh keep silence, nor think in itself of aught earthly; for the King of kings and Lord of lords cometh to be immolated, and to give Himself as food to the faithful. And before Him go the Angelic hosts, with their Principalities and Powers, the many-eyed Cherubim and the six-winged Seraphim, veiling their faces and loudly singing 'Alleluia.'"

The Liturgy ends with the blessing of bread, wine and oil, for the restauration of the worshippers' strength, for, according to ancient custom, they should spend this entire day and the night following on it in the church. After the service begins the reading of the Acts of the Apostles and continues until 10 p. m.

During the hour before midnight, all lampads and candelabra being lit, to the toll of the bells, the midnight service begins, during which the Canon for Holy Saturday is sung. When this service is concluded, the celebrants silently transport the "Sepulchre" from the middle of the church, through the Royal Gates into the Sanctuary, and there lay it upon the altar, where it remains until the end of the Paschal festival, in memory of Christ's forty days' sojourn on earth after His resurrection from the dead. Then all reverently await the stroke of midnight.

Special Features of the Services on the Day of the Holy Pascha.

At the stroke of twelve in the night from Saturday to Sunday, begins the celebration in honor of the Resurrection of Christ. This feast is called the Pascha,—by the name of the Old-Testament feast instituted in commemoration of the Jews' deliverance out of Egyptian bondage, because that feast was the prototype of the Christian feast. Then the blood of the lamb with which the doors of Hebrew dwellings were smeared preserved the Jews from the angel who was smiting the Egyptian first-born with death. Now Christ, in dying on the cross for our sins, like unto an immaculate Lamb, delivered us by His resurrection from the bondage of sin and the Devil. As we know of no event more joyful and radiant, the Church names this day "the Feast of Feasts" and "the triumph of triumphs." The substance of all the hymns of this feast is expressed in the Troparion "Christ is risen from the dead, overcoming death by death, and hath given life to them that lie in graves."

At midnight the celebrants, carrying the cross, the Testament and ikons, escorted and followed by all the faithful, to the ringing of the bells and the swinging of censers, go forth in procession and walk around the church on the outside, singing: "Thy resurrection, O Savior, angels sing in the heavens; vouchsafe that we also, on earth, may glorify Thee with pure hearts." The procession is to recall to us how the myrrh-bearing women went to the Sepulchre in the dim morning, intending to anoint the body of Christ with myrrh; it stops in the vestibule or on the porch before the western doors, which at this moment are closed. Here the priest blesses the beginning of Matins: "Glory to the holy, consubstantial, life-giving and undivided Trinity." In response to this the Troparion "Christ is risen" is sung many times. While the Troparion is being sung, the western doors are opened and the procession enters the church. The Matin service begins in the vestibule, in memory of the women having received the first news of the resurrection at the entrance of the Sepulchre. The entire Matin service consists of Ecteniæ and paschal hymns. First the Great Ectenia is recited; after that the entire Canon is sung, then the Irmi and the Troparia. Each Ode of the Canon ends with the Little Ectenia, and after each Ode every part of the church is censed. After the Canon the choir sings "Let all that hath breath praise the Lord," with verses, and the hymn "Let God arise" with Sticheræ. When the choir sings the Sticheræ: "Let us embrace one another, let us say 'Brethren' even to them that hate us, let us forgive all things for the sake of the Resurrection," all Christians exchange brotherly kisses, with the mutual greeting "Christ is risen"—"Verily He is risen." After which follow the Triple Ectenia, the Ectenia of Supplication, and dismissal.

The Hours offices consist exclusively of paschal hymns.

The Liturgy follows immediately after Matins. The Gospel Lesson read is one that tells not of the Resurrection of Christ, but of His pre-eternal birth from God the Father and of His Divinity, because Christ, by His resurrection, manifested His Divinity. It is customary, on this day, to read the Gospel in several languages, so that all may hear the glad tidings each in his own tongue.

Vespers also consist only of paschal hymns; the Introit is made with the Testament and the Gospel Lesson tells of the Resurrection.

The entire week is one feast. Therefore the services are alike on all days, with this only difference that, from Monday to Saturday, the procession takes place not in the beginning, but at the end of the Matin service, and no Gospel Lesson is read at Vespers. During the Paschal week all the doors of the Sanctuary remain open and the curtain drawn aside, in token that Christ, by His resurrection, hath opened to us the doors of the Kingdom of Heaven.

One of the special features of the Feast of the Pascha is the consecration of bread stamped with the image of the cross, or, sometimes, of the Resurrection, and named by the Greek name *Artos*. The Artos is consecrated at the close of the Paschal Liturgy in memory of Christ risen, Who is "the Bread of Life Eternal descended from Heaven and nourishing us with the food of His divine mercies." In memory of the visible sojourn of Christ upon earth after His resurrection, and of His constant invisible presence among the faithful, the Artos is carried around the church every day at the procession, then on Saturday, after the Liturgy, it is broken and distributed in the place of Antidoron among the faithful who partake of it on the spot only taking home pieces for those who were not present in church. This rite refers to the Apostles' custom of laying bread aside at their meals in memory of Christ, when He had ascended to Heaven. On the first Easter day the Church consecrates eggs, cheese and meat, thus proclaiming the end of Lent. In our country it is an immemorial custom to bring to the churches home-made Artos (large round loaves of rich, cake-like bread, called *Kulitch*) to be sprinkled with holy water, and for friends to exchange the gift of a red-dyed egg. The egg symbolizes the renovated life, received through the Blood of Christ Savior.

SPECIAL FEATURES OF THE SERVICES FROM THE PASCHAL WEEK TO ALL-SAINTS'-WEEK.

The Paschal hymns are sung through all the forty days until the Feast of the Ascension. The first Sunday after Easter is called the Sunday of the Apostle Thomas, also the Anti-Paschal, and the Renewal Sunday. The first name is given to this day because it is sacred to the memory of the Lord's appearing to the disciples, among whom was Thomas; the second and third names refer to the fact that on that day, for the first time after Easter Sunday, the celebration of the Resurrection is repeated and renewed. On the Tuesday of this week, and, in some localities, on the Monday also, a commemoration of the dead takes place, which is called a "joyful" one (*Rádonitsy*), because the prayers for the rest of the souls of the departed begin with the joyful tidings of the Resurrection. On the second Sunday the service is in honor of the Myrrh-bearing Women, Joseph of Arimathæa, and Nicodemus. The third Sunday commemorates the healing of the paralytic; the fourth—the talk with the Samaritan woman; the fifth—the healing of the man blind from birth. On Wednesday of the sixth week the Paschal festival is declared ended with closing prayers, and the singing of the Paschal hymns ceases.

The Thursday of the sixth week, which is the fortieth day from Easter Sunday, is sacred to the commemoration of the Ascension of Christ into Heaven.

The substance of the hymns for this day is expressed in the Troparion:—"Thou didst ascend in glory, O Christ our God, having gladdened the disciples with the promise of the Holy Ghost, of Whose coming they were assured by Thy blessing; for Thou art the Son of God, the Redeemer of the world.

On the fiftieth day after Easter Sunday and the tenth after the Ascension is celebrated the feast commemorating the Descent of the Holy Ghost upon the disciples of Christ. It is called the Feast of the Pentecost and lasts for two days. The first day of this feast is sacred to the honor and glory of the Most Holy Trinity and the memory of the descent of the Holy Ghost, and is called "Trinity-Day." The second day is celebrated in honor of the All-holy, life-giving, and All-mighty Spirit, and is called "Spirit-Day." The Church prepares for this feast by commemorating all the dead the day before. On Trinity-Day, Vespers follow immediately after the Liturgy, and at this service three prayers are offered, kneeling, that the Lord may send down to us the grace of the Holy Ghost and remember all the departed souls. It is customary to decorate the churches and houses on this day with trees and flowers and to stand at Vespers holding flowers. The trees and the flowers are offered to God as the first-fruits of summer, and remind us that Christians receive the renovation of their souls through the action of the Holy Ghost. In honor of this great feast, the Church dispenses from fasting on the Wednesday and Friday of the week following upon it.

Troparion for the day:—"Blessed art Thou, our God, that didst give us wise fishers of men, and didst send down upon them the Holy Ghost, and through them didst capture the universe. O Lover of men, glory to Thee."

The Sunday following on that of the Pentecost is consecrated to all the Saints, specially to those in whose honor no especial celebration has been instituted, on account of their numbers, or because of their names being unknown. With this day ends the series of movable services.

OF THE DIFFERENT MINISTRATIONS.

Administering the Sacraments of Baptism and Confirmation.

Baptism is the Sacrament in receiving which a person who believes in Christ, does, through immersion, thrice performed with the words: "The servant of God N. is baptized in the name of the Father and the Son and the Holy Ghost," die unto his or her former sinful life and receives the grace of the Holy Ghost, which confers a renovated and holy life.

Confirmation is the Sacrament in receiving which the person who has received baptism does, through the unction of the different parts of the body with holy chrism, with the words "the seal of the gift of the Holy Ghost," receive the grace of the Holy Ghost, confirming him or her in the renovated, Christian life. At present both these Sacraments are inseparable, and together form one church rite.

In view of the great importance of these two Sacraments in the life of a Christian, they are preceded by certain sacred acts which prepare persons to receive them worthily, and followed by other acts, impressing on the Christian the memory of their deep significance. To the former acts belong the rites of conferring a name, of doing reverence to the holy temple, and of reception among the Catechumens. The latter acts are: ablutions, tonsuring, and joining the Church.

Prayer for a Woman Who Hath Given Birth to a Child and Naming the Child.

At the present time it is customary to administer the Sacrament of Baptism to a child soon after its birth. Therefore the Orthodox Church cares for the babes of Christian parents as for her children. As soon as a child is born in a Christian family, a priest is called and prays, in the name of the entire Church, "that the Lord may preserve the mother and new born babe from all evil, shelter them under the covering of His wings, forgive the mother's trespasses, raise her from the bed of sickness, and vouchsafe that her babe may do reverence to His holy temple." The priest recites this prayer wearing the Epitrachelion (stole).

In obedience to the statutes of the Church, the babe, on the eighth day after birth, is brought before the doors of the temple, whereby its parents signify their desire that it should also be a Christian. Here it is met by the Priest, who blesses it (*signs it*) in the name of the Lord, gives it a Christian name, *i. e.* the name of some Saint, and prays to God "that the light of His countenance be signed on it; that it be signed with the cross of the only-begotten Son of God in its heart and understanding; that it may flee from the vanity of the world and every evil device of the Enemy and may keep God's commandments, and that the name of God may remain on it forever unrenounced." The babe is given a Christian name in token of its covenant with Christ, as a pledge that it may hope for salvation with the Saints, and as a reminder that it must emulate the life of the Saint whose name it bears. From this moment the babe enters the class of Catechumens, *i. e.* of those who are preparing to receive holy Baptism. In our country, the ceremony of naming is usually performed within the first days after birth, immediately after the prayer for the mother, and not before the door of a church, but at home, because the severity of the climate does not allow of carrying so young a babe out into the open air.

As the giving of a name is of great importance in a person's life, the day which is sacred to the memory of the Saint whose name he or she bears, is called a person's " name's day," and, to that person, is a festive one, on which he or she asks the help of God and the Saint towards leading a life worthy of that name. Christians look on their Saints as on their guardian angels; hence a person's " name's day " is also called his or her " angel's day."

Prayer on the Fortieth Day After Birth.

In imitation of the Virgin who, on the fortieth day after the birth of the Infant Jesus, brought Him to the temple, to present Him to the Lord, every Christian mother should bring her babe to church on the fortieth day after birth. The priest meets them in the vestibule, blesses mother and child, and prays that the Lord may bless them, purify and sanctify the mother and hold her worthy to partake of the Holy Eucharist,* and the babe borne by her to receive the Sacrament of Baptism.

The Rite of Reception Among the Catechumens.

This rite is performed just before baptism. The candidate for baptism is conducted or carried into the vestibule of the temple and stands before the font, looking towards the East, ungirdled, bareheaded and barefooted, with hands hanging down.

---

*The Church rules that a woman shall not partake of Holy Communion until the fortieth day after giving birth to a child, unless she be dangerously sick, even unto death.

By this ceremonial he betokens that he desires to cast off the old man and don a new man, after the image of Christ; that he aspires from darkness unto light, of which the East is the symbol, and humbly awaits illumination from Christ. The Priest breathes thrice in his face, blesses him and lays his hand upon his head. The priest's breath recalls the breath of life which the Creator breathed into the nostrils of the first created man, and betokens the breath of new life, imparted through the Sacrament of Baptism. The blessing in the name of Christ betokens separation from the community of the unbelieving, and the imposition of the hand—the entrance under the shelter of the Church. Laying his hand on the Catechumen's head, the Priest recites the preliminary prayer, in which he asks that the Lord may inscribe him in the Book of Life and receive him into His holy flock. This prayer is followed by the Catechumen rites: Exorcism,—the Renunciation of the Devil,—the Declaration of the desire to join Christ, the Profession of Faith, and the Adoration of the Holy Trinity.

In the Exorcisms the priest, in the name of the Almighty, commands the Devil to depart from the person who has been sealed with the name of the Lord Jesus Christ, and prays that God may expel the impure spirit from the Catechumen and make him a member of His holy Church. At the words "Drive from him every evil and unclean spirit hiding and lurking in his heart," the priest blows on the mouth, brow and breast of the Catechumen in token of the expulsion from his soul of all impurity.

After these prayers, the Catechumen is turned with his face towards the West, which symbolizes darkness and evil, and to the thrice repeated question, uttered by the Priest: " Dost thou renounce Satan and all his works, and all his angels, and all his service, and all his pomp?" he answers, with hands uplifted " I renounce." Then the Priest asks thrice " Hast thou renounced Satan?" and he answers " I have renounced," and, at the Priest's command, signifies, by blowing and spitting, his contempt of all things devilish.

Having renounced the Devil, the Catechumen turns again towards the East, with his hands down, and to the Priest's thrice repeated question "Dost thou join Christ?" he answers "I join." The priest again asks "Hast thou joined Christ?" He answers "I have joined." The priest then asks "And dost thou believe in Him?" to which the Catechumen answers "I believe in Him as King and God"—and forthwith recites the Creed. The last two questions the Priest utters thrice, and each time receives an affirmative answer, which is followed each time by the Creed.

Having received the Catechumen's renunciation of his former sinful life, the expression of his readiness to live with Christ and his profession of faith, the Priest commands him, as a new member of the Kingdom of Christ, "Bow thyself also unto Him." The Catechumen bows himself to the ground before the Holy Trinity, saying "I bow myself to the Father, and to the Son, and to the Holy Ghost, to the Trinity consubstantial and undivided."—The rite concludes with a prayer in which the Priest asks the Lord to count the Catechumen worthy to receive holy Baptism.

The same rite is performed over grown up candidates for baptism, and over infants. But as an infant cannot speak for itself, its sponsors answer for it. Both the Catechumen rites and that of Baptism are performed for grown up persons in a church, in the presence of the faithful. But in the case of infants, it is allowed to perform both at the parents' home, when the babe's weakness and the severity of the climate do not allow of taking it to church.

The Order of Baptism and Confirmation.

To perform the Sacrament of Baptism, the Priest puts on light-colored or white vestments, to express the joy of the Church at receiving a new member. Candles are lit around the edge of the font, the censer is swung, and the sponsors are given candles to hold. The lighted candles symbolize the spiritual illumination which is imparted through the Sacrament of Baptism, while the clouds of incense indicate the grace of the Holy Ghost, through whose operation man's regeneration takes place in this Sacrament.

The Order of Baptism consists of the consecration of the water, the anointing of the water and of the person baptized with consecrated oil, the immersion of the person into the water, the investing him with white garments, Confirmation (anointing with chrism or myrrh), the circumambulation of the font, and the reading of Lessons from the Holy Scriptures.

To the petitions of the Great Ectenia, with which the rite of Baptism begins, are added petitions " that the Lord may send down into this water the grace of redemption, so that the person baptized therein may become a child of light and an inheritor of the eternal blessings, grow one with Christ and become a partaker in His death and resurrection." The Priest then offers a prayer, " that the Lord may be present through the descent of the Holy Ghost and sanctify this water." At the words of the prayer, "Let all hostile powers be crushed beneath the sign of the image of Thy Cross," he blesses the water thrice and blows upon it. By this act he expresses his belief that the Devil is expelled by the name of Jesus Christ.

The water being consecrated, the priest proceeds to consecrate the oil by prayer, in token of reconciliation, and while "Alleluia" is being solemnly sung, he makes with the oil the sign of the cross on the water. Before this rite the admonition, " Let us attend ! " is uttered, to draw to it the attention of those present, and to signify that it conveys a mystical meaning. As water, which once upon a time submerged the entire human race, symbolizes purification, and oil gathered from the olive tree, a branch of which was brought to Noah in the ark by the dove, in token of reconciliation, symbolizes mercy, so the combination of both these symbols signifies that the purification of man by the waters of baptism takes place through the mercy of God.

Having thus prepared the material for the Sacrament, the Priest now proceeds to prepare for it the person about to receive it. He anoints the brow, ears, breast, hands and feet with the consecrated oil, in token that, through baptism, man, like unto a branch of the wild olive tree, is grafted unto the good olive tree, which is Christ. As man dies in baptism to his former life and comes forth a new man to battle with evil, so the anointing with oil serves him, as one dead, as a preparation to sepulture and, as a soldier of Christ—as a preparation to the struggle with iniquity.

The act of baptism itself is performed by the thrice repeated immersion of the recipient of the Sacrament into the water, with the words, "The servant (or handmaid) of God N. is baptized in the name of the Father, and the Son, and the Holy Ghost, now and ever, and to the ages of ages; amen." During the immersion he who is baptized is turned to the East. At this moment the grace of the Holy Ghost descends on him and gives him a new life, washing away all sins from his soul; while being immersed, he is entombed with Christ; when lifted out of the water, he rises with Him. The blessings which man receives in the Sacrament of Baptism are expressed in the words of the Psalm (31) which is sung immediately after the immersion: "Blessed are they whose transgressions are forgiven, whose sin is covered. Blessed is the man to whom the Lord imputeth not iniquity . . . Many sorrows shall be to the wicked; but he that trusteth in the Lord, mercy shall compass him about. Be glad in the Lord and rejoice, ye righteous; and shout for joy all ye that are upright in heart."

In token of the purity of the neophyte's soul the Priest invests him with a white garment, calling it, "the robe of righteousness," and in token that he shall live after baptism, he places round his neck a cross, the symbol of walking after Christ. During the robing, a Troparion is sung, indicating the meaning of the white garment: "Give unto me a shining robe, Thou that art invested with light as with a garment, O most merciful Christ, our God."

As special help from God is needed to follow after Christ and preserve the soul's purity, obtained through baptism, the Sacrament of Confirmation is administered to the neophyte immediately after the robing. The Priest makes the sign of the cross with consecrated chrism on his brow, eyes, nostrils, lips, ears, breast, hands and feet, saying each time, "The seal of the gift of the Holy Ghost." Through this unction is imparted the grace of the Holy Ghost, which confirms in the new life and gives the strength to live in Christ.

The Priest now walks three times around the font with the neophyte and sponsors, to the chant: "As many as have been baptized into Christ, have put on Christ." The circumambulation of the font signifies the triumph and joy of the Church, because a Christian has been joined with Christ forever.

The Order of the Sacrament concludes with a Lesson from the Epistle, in which the meaning of baptism is set forth, also the benefits bestowed by this Sacrament, and the duties which it imposes on us,—and with a Lesson from the Gospel, on the institution of the Sacrament by Jesus Christ.

Note 1st.—OF BAPTISM PERFORMED BY A LAYMAN.— The right to administer the Sacrament of Baptism belongs to the priests. But in an emergency, when no priest is to be had, and the candidate for baptism is feeble, and there is danger of his dying before he can be baptized, any layman has the right, and indeed the duty, to perform the rite by thrice repeated immersion, or even by aspersion, or by pouring of water on the head, with the words "the servant (or handmaid) of God N. is baptized in the name of the Father and the Son and the Holy Ghost, now and ever and to the ages of ages; amen." Such a baptism is entirely valid. Later on, the priest does not repeat the rite, but only completes it by saying the omitted prayers and performing the omitted rites, then enters it into the church register.

Note 2d. THE SPONSORS.—At every baptism, whether of a grown up person or of an infant, sponsors are absolutely necessary. If the former, they serve as witnesses of the neophyte's profession of faith and the vows he takes; if the latter, they answer all questions for the infant. After baptism they assume the spiritual care of the neophyte, and are bound to be his guides in Christian life and to see to his religious education. Through these duties a spiritual relationship is established between the sponsors and their god-child, also the latter's parents; the sponsors are god-fathers and god-mothers. As the sponsors assume important responsibilities towards their godchildren, the Church rules that they shall have attained the age of discretion—(the godfather to be not under 15, the godmother not under 13)—that they shall be persons of good moral standing, with a knowledge of the fundamental doctrines of the Orthodox Church, and themselves Orthodox. Persons of other Christian confessions are permitted to take part in the rite of baptism as "honorary persons," but in that case it is absolutely necessary that the god-father should be Orthodox if the neophyte is of the male sex, or the god-mother, if of the female sex. Parents may not be sponsors for their own children; nor may monks or nuns be sponsors.

THE RITES OF ABLUTION AND TONSURE.

In ancient times neophytes did not lay aside their white garments for seven days, nor wash the spots on their bodies which had been anointed with holy chrism; and, that the seal laid on them by the unction might not be effaced, they wore wreaths or bandages. On the eighth day they came to church, and there the Priest loosed the girdle of their garments, removed the bandage from their brow and washed the anointed parts. At present this ablution is performed immediately after the reading of the Gospel Lesson. The Priest first prays to God, that the neophyte may not defile the spiritual garment of incorruption given him at baptism, nor break the spiritual seal laid upon him through the Sacrament of Confirmation; then he sprinkles the neophyte with water, reminding him that he is, "justified, illuminated, confirmed, sanctified and washed in the name of Jesus Christ and by the Spirit of our God"; after which he wipes with a sponge the anointed parts of his body, reminding him that he is "baptized, illuminated, confirmed, sanctified, and washed in the name of the Most Holy Trinity."

Immediately after the ablution, the tonsure of the hair is performed. It was customary among the ancient Hebrews to shear the hair and burn it on the altar in token of entire self-consecration to God. This ancient custom passed into the Christian Church. Christians shear the hair of newborn infants in token that, having received baptism, they have become citizens of the Kingdom of God on earth, and have consecrated themselves to the service of God, before Whom they have promised to cut away from their souls sinful thoughts and passions. After the ablution the Priest performs the tonsure in the name of the Most Holy Trinity, praying that God may help the neophyte to become learned in His law and to live according to that law.

THE RITE OF JOINING THE CHURCH.

The neophyte has now the right to enter the church, to take part in all the prayers and to partake of the Holy Eucharist. The first time he comes to church, he does so with some solemnity and this act is called, "joining the Church," (*i. e.* "being admitted into the community of Christians.") The Priest meets the neophyte at the entrance of the church, takes him or her on his arms and after making the sign of the cross before the main door, says: "The servant (or handmaid) of God N. is admitted to join the Church in the name of the Father, and the Son, and the Holy Ghost, now and ever and unto the ages of ages; amen." Then he leads or carries the neophyte into the church with the words, "He (or she) entereth into Thy house to worship in Thy holy temple." Pausing in the middle of the church, he repeats the words of admission, and adds: "In the midst of the church he shall sing unto Thee." Once again he repeats the words of admission before the Royal Gates, and, if the neophyte be of the male sex, leads or carries him into the sanctuary; if of the female sex, he brings her only as far as the Royal Gates, and repeats the prayer of St. Simeon, "Lord, now lettest Thou Thy servant depart in peace . . ." Then he gives up the neophyte to the sponsors.

As infants, at the present day, are usually baptized before the fortieth day after birth, the rite of their admission into the church usually takes place the fortieth day, when the mother brings her babe herself to present it to the Lord and to receive herself the permission to partake of holy communion. Formerly a mother used to receive communion on that day and the child also receives it then for the first time. The latter custom prevails to this day.

The Sacrament of Baptism properly performed, cannot be repeated, that of Confirmation can be repeated only for such persons as having renounced the faith of Christ and adopted Paganism, Mohammedanism or Judaism, again return to Christ.

THE RITE OF ADMISSION INTO THE ORTHODOX CHURCH OF FOLLOWERS OF OTHER CHRISTIAN CONFESSIONS.

Heterodox Christians, who have received the Sacrament of Baptism, but not that of Confirmation, are admitted into the Orthodox Church by administering the Sacrament, and declaring them Catechumens. The person seeking admission confesses his sins before a priest, but does not receive absolution. Then, in the vestibule (or, where there is none, by the western entrance), he abjures all his former errors of faith and professes the doctrine of the Orthodox Church. The Priest then conducts him into the church, saying: "Enter into the Church of God and cast away all wrongs and errors." He kneels in the middle of the church before a lectern, upon which lie a cross and Testament, and hears a prayer in which the Priest beseeches the Lord to grant that this man may irrevocably, without deceit or guile, be joined unto the Holy Church Catholic. After this prayer he rises and pledges himself under oath: "Firmly to maintain and profess the Orthodox faith, with the help of God, whole and intact, to his last breath, and to fulfill all its obligations," and, in affirmation of this promise, kisses the cross and Testament. After taking the oath, he kneels once more, and the Priest pronounces over him the prayer of remission and absolution, anoints him with the holy chrism and places a cross around his neck. The rite concludes with the Ectenia, in which the sponsors are prayed for, and dismissed.

If the person admitted has already been confirmed in his own Church, he is not anointed, but the Priest admits him through imposition of hands.

THE RITE OF ANOINTING TSARS AT THEIR CORONATION.

The Anointing of a Tsar is a sacred act by which the grace of the Holy Ghost is imparted to him, to fit him for the performance of the highest ministry on earth. The entire rite consists of two acts: the coronation, and the anointing with holy chrism. In Russia this rite is performed in Moscow, in the Church of the Assumption.

The order of the ceremonies is as follows: First a Te-Deum is sung for the health of their Imperial Majesties, followed by the Office of the Hours. During this service the imperial regalia are brought into the church,— the purple mantle, the crown, the sceptre and the orb. Bishops in full pontificals meet them with incense and asperse them with holy water, and remain near the entrance, in readiness to receive their Imperial Majesties. When the Emperor and Empress enter the church, one of the Metropolitans greets them and offers them the cross to kiss while another sprinkles them with holy water. Their Majesties then proceed into the church, preceded by the Bishops, perform a prostration before the Royal Gates, kiss the principal ikons, then, ascending the dais, seat themselves on the thrones prepared for them in the middle of the church, while the bishops station themselves in two lines from the throne to the Royal Gates. During this time Psalm 100 is sung, "Of mercy and judgment I will sing unto Thee, O Lord..."

THE EMPEROR'S CROWN.

THE EMPRESS' CROWN.

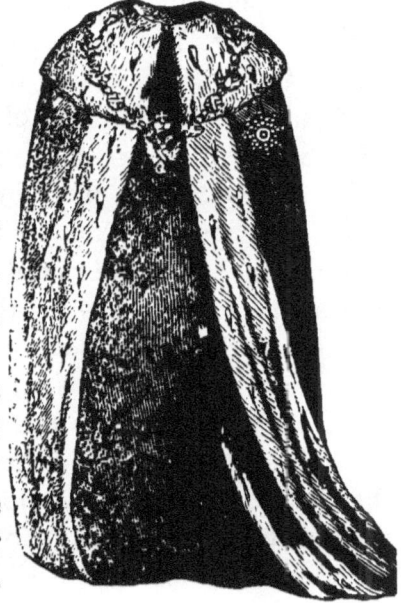
THE IMPERIAL PURPLE.

When their Majesties have taken their seats, the presiding Metropolitan ascends the imperial dais and asks the Emperor what faith he professes. The Emperor replies by reciting the Creed in a loud voice.

After this public profession of faith by the Emperor, the rite of coronation begins. After the hymn, "O Heavenly King," has been sung, the Great Ectenia is recited with the addition of petitions for a prosperous reign. Then are sung the hymn, "God is the Lord..." and the Troparion, "Save, O Lord, Thy people..." followed by a Parœmia and Lessons from the Gospels and Epistle. The Parœmia speaks of the Divine protection extended over the Tsar; the Epistle Lesson—of obedience to Kings; the Gospel Lesson—of the tribute to Cæsar. After the reading of the Gospel Lesson, the Emperor is invested with the purple and the chain of the Order of the Apostle Andrew the First-called, presented by the Metropolitan, with the words, "In the name of the Father, and the Son, and the Holy Ghost." Having received the purple, the Emperor inclines his head, the Metropolitan signs it with the cross, by laying his hands on it crosswise, and prays that the Lord may anoint the Tsar with the oil of gladness, invest him with strength, crown him with precious stones, grant him length of days, place in his right hand the sceptre of salvation, seat him on the throne of righteousness, keep him under His shelter and establish his rule." After this prayer the Emperor takes the crown from the cushion presented by the Metropolitan and places it upon his head, while the Metropolitan again utters the words, "In the name of the Father, and the Son and the Holy Ghost." After the Emperor has assumed the crown, the Metropolitan explains the meaning of the coronation rite: "This visible and material adornment of thy head is to thee a manifest sign that the King of Glory, Christ, invisibly crowneth thee, the head of the throne of All the Russias." Then, from a cushion presented by the Metropolitan, the Emperor takes in his right hand the sceptre and in his left the orb (a small globe, symbolizing the

THE ORB.

THE SCEPTRE

lands subject to him), while the Metropolitan again utters the words, "In the name of the Father, and the Son, and the Holy Ghost." Then the Metropolitan tells the Emperor the meaning of the sceptre and orb, as follows: "God-crowned, God-given, God-adorned, most pious Autocrat and great Sovereign, Emperor of All the Russias! Receive the sceptre and the orb, which are the visible signs of the autocratic power given thee from the Most High over thy people, that thou mayest rule them and order for them the welfare they desire." Having assumed the imperial regalia, the Emperor seats himself upon the throne, and laying the sceptre and orb on a cushion presented to him by dignitaries, calls to him Her Majesty the Empress. Her Majesty rises from her throne and kneels before the Emperor, who takes the crown from his head and touches with it the Empress' head, then replaces the crown on his own head and places on her's a smaller crown, presented by a dignitary. Then the Empress is invested with the purple and the chain of St. Andrew, and seats herself on her throne. A Deacon proclaims, "length of days to their Majesties," (as at the service of the Royal Hours), after which the Emperor kneels down and, in a loud voice, offers a prayer in which he beseeches the Lord as follows: "Instruct me in the work on which Thou hast sent me, grant me wisdom and direct me for this great ministry." The rite of coronation concludes with a prayer offered by the Metropolitan, all present kneeling and with the singing of the hymn, "Thee, O God, we praise." After this hymn the Liturgy begins.

THE SWORD.

It is during the Liturgy that the rite of anointing takes place. As the Liturgy begins, the Emperor puts away the crown. After the Gospel Lesson, the Testament is presented to their Majesties to kiss. When the communion hymn has been sung, the Emperor gives his sword to a dignitary, and walks, mantled, to the Royal Gates, which, at this moment are thrown open. The Empress follows him and stops midway between the throne and the Ambo.

Two Metropolitans step out of the Sanctuary. The presiding Metropolitan anoints the Emperor with holy chrism on the brow, the eyes, the nostrils, the lips, the ears, the breast, and the hands—palm and back—saying every time, "the seal of the gift of the Holy Ghost;" the other Metropolitan wipes off the chrism with cotton. Then the Emperor steps aside and stands at the right side of the Royal Gates, next to the ikon of the Savior. The Empress now approaches the Royal Gates, and the presiding Metropolitan anoints her with holy chrism, on the brow only, with the words, "the seal of the gift of the Holy Ghost," when the Empress steps aside and stands at the left side of the Royal Gates, next to the ikon of the Mother of God.

After the rite of anointing has been performed, their Majesties receive holy communion. The Metropolitan conducts the Emperor, through the Royal Gates, into the Sanctuary, and there, at the altar, gives him the Eucharist, as to the Anointed of God and the supreme protector of the Christian Church, after the rite for the clergy,—*i. e.* he places in his hand a portion of the Body of Christ, then lets him partake of the Blood of Christ from the chalice. The Empress receives communion in the usual manner before the Royal Gates. After receiving communion, their Imperial Majesties resume their seats on the thrones, where, after the prayers of thanksgiving and for length of days have been said, they receive the loyal congratulations of churchmen and laymen.

THE ORDER OF THE CONSECRATION OF A CHURCH.

The material church is the visible image of the spiritual body called, "the Church of Christ," the Head of which is Christ, and the members are all who believe in Christ. Therefore, as every human being enters into the Church through the Sacraments of Baptism and Confirmation, so every new church becomes a House of God, for the dispensing within its walls of the gifts of the grace of the Holy Ghost, only after it has been consecrated by means of certain sacred offices, which bear some similitude to the Sacraments of Baptism and Confirmation.

Rite at the Laying of the Foundation of a Church.

This rite is performed at the laying of the foundation, and consists of the placing of the foundation stone. The Bishop, or a priest deputed by him, comes with cross and ikons to the spot dug for the foundation. The service begins with a Te-Deum and consecration of water; then, to the singing of appropriate Troparia in honor of the person in whose name the church is to be built, the Bishop or Priest censes around the spot and offers a prayer, wherein he asks that "the Lord may keep the builders of the temple unharmed and the foundations thereof unimpaired, and that He may help the completion thereof unto the glory of God." After this prayer he takes a square-cut stone, (a cube), in which is engraven a cross, and under the cross is a hollow place to hold sacred relics, sprinkles the stone with holy water, and having made with it the sign of the cross, places it in the foundation with the words: "The Most High laid this foundation, God abideth in the midst of it and it shall not be removed, and God shall support it from day to day." Upon the stone is laid a metallic plate with an inscription, setting forth in whose honor the church is founded, and giving the names of the reigning Emperor, the local Bishop, and the persons at whose expense the church is to be built, and also the name of the Saint whose relics—if any, are deposited in the foundation.

After this ceremony, the Bishop or Priest plants a wooden cross on the spot where the altar is to stand, with a prayer, "that the Lord may bless and sanctify this spot by the force and operation of the precious and life-giving tree of the Cross." On the cross there also is an inscription, setting forth in whose name the altar is consecrated, under the reign of what Emperor, and with what Bishop's blessing, also in what year, month and date the foundation was laid.

The Rite of the Consecration of a Church.

On the eve of the consecration of a newly-built church an All-night Vigil is celebrated before the sanctuary, with the Royal Gates closed.

The consecration itself is performed in different ways, according to who the consecrator is—a Bishop, or a priest deputed by a Bishop.

Consecration by a Bishop.—The following preparations for the consecration are made: Before the Royal Gates, upon a table covered with a white linen cloth, are placed: a Testament, a cross, the sacred vessels, the spoon, the lance, the veils, the aërs, the cloths with which the altar and the Table of Oblations are to be dressed, a rope for fastening the altar, and nails. Around this table are placed four candlesticks. In the Sanctuary near the Bema are placed upon a separate table, the holy chrism, rose water, the twig for anointing with chrism, an aspergill, and some stones. Before the ikon of the Savior in the screen (*ikonostas*), upon a lectern, are placed the sacred relics, on a paten, covered with the asterisk and aër.

On the day of consecration, the sacred relics are transferred to the nearest church and there placed upon the altar. If there is no church near enough, they remain where they are, before the ikon of the Savior.

The rite of consecration begins with a Te-Deum with consecration of water, after which the celebrants put on full vestments, and, over them, a wide and long apron, tied round the neck and waist, and under the arms, then carry the table with the church belongings into the Sanctuary; this done, the Royal Gates are closed.

When the Royal Gates are closed and all persons who are not participants in the ceremony have gone out of the sanctuary, the altar is established, thus: The Bishop sprinkles with holy water the props of the altar, then pours into the hollows prepared for the nails some cero-mastix (a preparation of wax mixed with sundry fragrant and adhesive substances, incense and white sulphur), and sprinkles the top board of the altar, the nails and stones. Thereupon the priests lay the top board upon the props and hammer in the nails with the stones. During all these proceedings Psalms are sung. When the altar is established, the Royal Gates are opened, and the Bishop, kneeling, offers a prayer that the Lord may send down the Holy Ghost and sanctify the temple and altar. He then re-enters the Sanctuary and the Royal Gates are closed once more.

Then begins the ablution of the altar. To the singing of psalms, the Bishop rubs the board with soap in the form of a cross, and pours upon it tepid water, which has been sanctified by prayer, when the priests take cloths and rub the altar dry. Then he takes red wine mixed with rose water, pours the mixture upon the altar in the shape of a cross and rubs it in, wherein he is assisted by the priests. With the same wine he sprinkles the Antimins prepared for the new church. The priests take sponges sprinkled with holy water and wipe off the altar. This ceremony of ablution is symbolical of the altar's high significance. The tepid water symbolizes the grace of the Holy Ghost, which warms the hearts of the faithful; the rosewater recalls the precious myrrh brought by the women for Christ's entombing, while the red wine signifies the Blood of Christ, shed for our salvation.

After the ablution, the Bishop anoints with holy chrism the top board and the props, as also the Antimins prepared for the altar. Then begins the vesting of the altar: First in a white cover, which is tied to the altar, cross-wise, with the rope; over this first cover a second one, of brilliant material, is slipped; (it is called *endyton*, i. e. " covering," " garment "—a Greek word); then on the altar is laid the *eilyton* (" wrap," also a Greek word), and in that the Antimins is enfolded. All these articles are put in place after having been sprinkled with holy water, to the chanting of a psalm. This completes the consecration of the altar, after which the Bishop and priest put away the aprons, and the Royal Gates are opened.

The Bishop now proceeds to the consecration of the church. Preceded by candle-bearers, while a psalm is chanted, he walks around the whole church, censing it as he goes; two priests follow him; one sprinkles the wall with holy water, and the other anoints with chrism the wall above the Bema, above the western door, and the northern and southern wall above the doors and windows. Re-entering the Sanctuary, the Bishop lights a light on the Bema; from this all the candles and lamps are lit.

After the consecration the Bishop goes in procession, while Troparia are chanted, in honor of the martyrs, to the nearest church, to bring thence the holy relics. There, approaching the altar, upon which the relics are reposing, he prays, kneeling, that the Lord, hearing the holy martyrs' prayers, may grant us a share in His inheritance; then he censes the holy relics, takes the paten containing them upon his head, and, thus carrying them, returns in procession to the newly built church and walks around it on the outside, to the singing of Troparia on the upbuilding and establishing of the Church of the Savior, at the same time sprinkling the external walls with holy water. Then he stops before the western entrance, places the paten with the relics on a lectern, and blesses his assistant celebrants. Thereupon the choir enters the church and the doors are closed after them. The processional circumambulation of the church signifies that the building is consecrated to God forever.

Note.—If the holy relics were in the newly built church itself, the Bishop takes them on his head, to the singing of Troparia in honor of the martyrs, and having offered the prayer, goes forth and carries them in procession around the church. If this is not possible, the Bishop, having taken up the holy relics, places them on a lectern before the western door of the church, or before a curtain hung up temporarily in the place of that door.

Standing before the closed door of the church, the Bishop calls out, " Lift up your heads, O ye gates; and be ye lift up, ye everlasting doors; and the King of Glory shall come in." The choir, from within the church, sing in reply, " Who is this King of Glory?" While these words are sung, the Bishop censes the relics. Then he calls out again, "Lift up your heads, O ye gates; and be ye lift up, ye everlasting doors; and the King of Glory shall come in." Again the choir reply from within the church, "Who is this King of Glory?" The Bishop here offers a prayer, "that the Lord may stablish the newly built temple and let it endure unto the end of time." Then he takes up the paten with the holy relics, and, making with it the sign of the cross before the entrance, calls out, "The Lord of hosts, He is the King of Glory." These words are repeated by the choir, within the church. At this moment the doors are thrown open, and the Bishop enters in procession, bearing the paten with the relics on his head, places it on the altar, anoints a particle of the relics with chrism, places it in a small casket which he fills with cero-mastix, and which a priest, having taken it from him, and closed down the lid, deposits inside the central prop of the altar; the other particle of the holy relics the Bishop deposits in the Antimins, after having also anointed it with chrism. When the holy relics have been deposited in their places, a prayer is offered for the builders of the church and dismissal of the consecration is made, after which follow the Hours and the Liturgy.

The Rite of the Consecration of a Church by a Priest.— The special features of the consecration of a church when performed by a priest are the following: 1) It is not a paten with holy relics which is placed on a lectern before the ikon of the Savior, but an Antimins, consecrated beforehand by a Bishop and containing holy relics; 2) at the establishing of the altar, the prescribed psalms are sung, but no prayer is offered, as that was offered by the Bishop at the consecration of the Antimins; 3) at the ablution of the altar, it is not washed with red wine and rosewater, as this act was performed by the Bishop with the Antimins; 4) the altar is fastened with the rope not crosswise, but in the usual way; 5) the walls are not anointed with chrism; 6) it is the Antimins which is carried in procession around the church; 7) no holy relics are placed inside the prop under the altar.

THE RITE OF CONFESSION.

When a Christian falls into sin after baptism, he violates the vows he took at baptism, separates himself from the Church, and forfeits the right to partake of holy communion. But there remains to him the possibility of cleansing himself again from sins and being saved; for Jesus Christ gave to His disciples the power of remitting the sins of those who repented and of again joining them to His Church. This power the Apostles transmitted to their successors, the Bishops, and these again empowered the priests to hear the repentant confessions of the faithful and to remit their sins in the name of Jesus Christ, if they judged that their repentance was sincere and strong. This remission of sins is given in the Sacrament of Penance which is therefore called a "second baptism," a "baptism by tears," and the office in which it is performed is called the " Rite of Confession."

The Sacrament of Penance is one in which the Christian who confesses his sins before the entire Church or her representative, and sues for pardon, receives absolution from the Priest, and at the same moment is invisibly absolved by Christ Himself. Hence the rite of Confession consists of three acts: prayers for the remission of sins; confession of sins before the priest; and absolution from sins in the name of Jesus Christ.

After hearing the preliminary prayers, the penitential Troparia, the Penitential Psalm and the prayers for the remission of sins, the penitent, standing before the ikon of the Savior, confesses his sins to the Priest, concealing nothing, adducing no excuses to minimize his transgressions, then asks for pardon and absolution. After confession he kneels and bows his head. The priest then prays that the Lord may forgive the penitent's sins and join him to His holy Church, covers his head with the Epitrachelion (stole) in token that he, the priest, through the grace of God, has the power to remit sins in the name of Jesus Christ, blesses him, and utters the words of absolution: " Our Lord and God, Jesus Christ, by His grace and the bountifulness of His lovingkindness, forgive thee, child, N., all thy transgressions; and I, an unworthy priest, by His power which is given unto me, forgive thee and absolve thee from all thy sins, in the name of the Father, and the Son, and the Holy Ghost, amen." With these words the grace of the Holy Ghost descends into the soul of the penitent and cleanses it of sins, so that he, by the grace of God, goes from the presence of the Priest a pure and holy man.

As only he receives remission of sins who, repenting of them, profoundly regrets having committed them and firmly determines to abstain from them in the future, such repentance necessitates a period of preparation. During this time the Christian lays aside all worldly pre-occupations, and devotes himself to fasting, prayer, meditation on his soul, and the better to do all this, seeks solitude and keeps away from all amusements and distracting things. The length of the time of preparation depends on how long a time a man can spare from his worldly obligations.

The priest who receives a penitent's confession enters into a close spiritual connection with him, and therefore is called his "spiritual father," while the penitent is the priest's "spiritual child." The spiritual father does not merely hear the sinner's confession and judge of the condition of his soul; he, like a physician, tries to find out what is his spiritual disease, points out to the careless transgressor how important and deep-seated his sins are, and him who despairs of his improvement and salvation he supports and encourages by hope in the mercy of God. This means that the better the spiritual father knows his spiritual children, the more useful his counsels and instructions will be to them. It is a rule, therefore, that a spiritual father shall not be changed without absolute necessity.

It sometimes happens that a spiritual father remits a penitent's sins on condition that he will fulfill some task or discipline imposed upon him, either of prohibition or command, this is called a "penance." The spiritual father imposes a penance to help the penitent to break himself of a sinful habit, or to cure him of carelessness with regard to his self-correction, or again to calm his conscience troubled by sin and not let him sink into despair. The penance imposed by one spiritual father cannot be remitted by another, excepting in case of the penitent's dangerous illness or that of the death of the spiritual father himself.

THE RITE OF THE SACRAMENT OF ORDERS.

The Sacrament of Orders is that in which one who has been canonically selected and ordained by a Bishop receives the grace of the Holy Ghost and is instituted to perform the Sacraments and tend the flock of Christ, *i. e.* to govern a Christian church. As the grace of the Holy Ghost is imparted in this Sacrament through the imposition of the prelate's hands, the act of performing the sacrament is named the *Cheirotony*, which means in Greek, the "stretching out" or "laying on of hands." The rite is the same for all grades of priesthood—that of Bishop, Presbyter, or Deacon, differing only in that it is performed at different moments of the Liturgy. It consists of the following acts: presentation of the person selected for holy orders, circumambulation of the altar, the prayer of consecration, the laying on of hands, and vesting with the sacred vestments.

The Ordering of a Deacon.

As the deacon does not perform the Sacrament of the Eucharist, but only ministers thereat, his ordination takes place after the consecration of the Holy Gifts. Two sub-deacons conduct the deacon-elect from the middle of the church before the Bishop, who is seated on a throne at the left of the altar, and the deacons utter the words: " Bid ye and ye, and thou, Right Reverend Master." The first "bid" is addressed to the people, the second to the clergy, the third to the Bishop. This indicated that in ancient times the people and clergy as well as the Bishop took part in the election of persons to be ordered for sacred functions. The deacon-elect bows himself to the ground before the Bishop and receives his blessing. Then the deacons lead him twice around the altar in token that he vows to devote himself forever to the service of the church. During this act he kisses the corners of the altar in token of reverence for God, and after each circumambulation bows himself to the ground before the bishop, and kisses his hand and Thigh-shield (*pálitsa*) in token of submissiveness to his authority. All through this ceremony are sung the following sacred hymns: " O ye holy martyrs, who valiantly contended and received the crown, pray to the Lord that our souls may be saved."—" Glory to Thee, Christ God, the Apostles' boast and the martyrs' joy, who preached the consubstantial Trinity."—" Rejoice, O Isaiah! the Virgin is with child and bringeth forth a son, Emmanuel, God and man, the Orient is his name, whom magnifying, we call the Virgin blessed."*) After the circumambulation, the deacon-elect kneels down before the altar, but on only the right knee, because he does not receive the full ordination of priesthood, and lays his hands and forehead upon the altar, in token of consecration to God of all his faculties. Then the Bishop, rising from the throne, covers the candidate's head with the ends of his Omophorion, blesses him, lays his hand upon his head, and speaks the prayer of ordination: "The Divine grace, which ever healeth what is infirm and supplieth what is wanting, passing through my hand, ordereth this most pious Sub-deacon for Deacon; let us therefore pray for him, that the grace of the All-holy Spirit may come on him." The assistant celebrants in the Sanctuary sing thrice, "Lord have mercy!" and the choir responds " *Kyrie eleison,*" ("Lord have mercy" in Greek), to indicate that our Russian Church received the cheirotony of priesthood from the Greek Church, and to this day preserves intact the bond that unites them. During the prayer of ordination the recipient of

---

*These hymns indicate that the person receiving holy orders must, in his life and in the exercise of his functions, follow the example of the martyrs; that his preaching must have for its subject the doctrine of the Holy Trinity and that of the Incarnation of the Son of God from a virgin, which was the foundation of the Church and the Priesthood.

the Sacrament receives the grace of the Holy Ghost, which ordereth him for a sacred ministry. After the laying on of hands, the Bishop delivers to the newly ordained deacon the vestments and signs of his office: the Orarion, the maniples, and the fan, uttering the Greek word *"Axios"* ("worthy") which is repeated by the choir in the name of the people and clergy. Having received the fan, the newly ordained Deacon takes his stand at the left side of the altar and fans the Holy Gifts, calling to mind as he does so that he must minister at the altar of God with the same reverence with which the holy angels minister to God Himself. At the same Liturgy the newly ordained Deacon receives communion and recites the Ectenia of thanksgiving at the close of the Liturgy.

The Ordering of a Presbyter.

The deacon who is to be ordained priest is led out by deacons into the middle of the church, before the Bishop, after the singing of the Cherubic Hymn, in order that he may on the same day take part in the celebration of the Eucharist. The circumambulation of the altar is conducted by a priest. The candidate bends both knees before the altar, in token that he takes upon himself the greater ministry, and for that end is to receive the highest gift of priesthood. After the prayer of ordination, the Bishop gives to the newly ordained priest the vestments of his office: the Epitrachelion (stole), the girdle and the Phelonion (cope) and places in his hands the Book of Offices (manual of church services). The newly ordained priest then takes part in the further celebration of the Liturgy. After the transmutation of the Holy Gifts, the Bishop presents to him a portion of the Lamb, with the words:—" Receive this pledge and preserve it whole and intact unto thy latest breath, for thou shalt be held to account for it at the second and dread coming of our Lord, and God, and Savior, Jesus Christ."—This ceremony indicates that the priest is the performer of the Holy Sacraments and that it is his duty to guard their sacredness, admitting to participate in them only them that are worthy. Before the exclamation "The Holy to the holy,' this pledge is returned to the Bishop. The newly ordained priest then receives holy communion and reads the prayer for which the celebrant descends from the Ambo.

The Ordering of a Bishop.

The consecration of a bishop takes place at the beginning of the Liturgy, since a bishop has the right not only of performing the Sacrament of the Eucharist, but also of ordaining deacons and priests; moreover it is performed not by one bishop but by several, i. e. by a convention of bishops. Before the beginning of the Liturgy, an arch-priest and a deacon conduct the candidate to an Ambo (or platform) placed in the middle of the church, where the bishops are seated. Here, standing on an *Orlets* (" Eaglet " or eagle-rug)* he recites the Creed, expounds in detail the doctrine of the properties of the persons of the Holy Trinity and of the Incarnation of the Son of God, then pledges himself to observe the canons of the Apostles and Councils, the traditions of the Church, and to obey the Most Holy Synod, and, lastly, takes two oaths: the general State oath of allegiance and single-hearted service to the throne and obedience to the Emperor and the laws by him issued,—and a special oath instituted for spiritual authorities, of fulfilling their duties in all conscience and the fear of God. Having taken both oaths, he receives the blessing of the oldest bishop present and kisses the hands of the other bishops who are to consecrate him.

After the Introit with the Testament, the arch-priest and deacon conduct the bishop-elect before the Royal Gates. Here he is met by the bishops and kneels before the altar on both knees. The bishops lay an open Testament, text downward, upon his head, as though it were the hand of Christ Savior, and hold it there. During this time the oldest bishop says the prayer of consecration; after which the bishops chant "Lord have mercy," and lay their right hands upon the head of the bishop-elect.

*See pp. 28 and 31.

This ends the consecration, and the new bishop is forthwith robed in the Saccos and Omophorion, during which act the word *"Axios"* is uttered loudly. Then he takes part in the celebration of the Liturgy. When the Liturgy is ended, the oldest of the bishops present the newly consecrated bishop with the crozier. This is done on the Ambo in the middle of the church.

Note 1.—THE CONSECRATION OF CLERICS AND ACOLYTES:—These persons, when they enter the service of the Church, do not receive holy orders, but only a bishop's blessing. The Bishop lays his hands on their heads, but does not pray for the grace of the Holy Ghost. The imposition of hands is not called *cheirotony*, but *cheirothesis*. It usually takes place after the robing of the Bishop, before the reading of the Hours. The Bishop blesses the person chosen for Reader or Lampadary (candle-bearer), lays his hand upon his head, and says a prayer, in which he asks God to help him to perform his ministry worthily, then tonsures him in the shape of a cross in the name of the Father and the Son and the Holy Ghost. After this he puts on a short Phelonion, and is given the book of the Epistle, from which he reads a few lines. Then the *phelonion* is taken from him; he puts on a Sticharion (tunic) and is given a lampad, (a tall candlestick) which he holds, standing through the Liturgy. The book and the lampad are given him as insignia of his ministry.

When a reader is consecrated for sub-deacon, the Bishop girds him over the Sticharion with an Orarion and laying his hands on him, says a prayer, after which the newly consecrated sub-deacon receives a towel and basin, in token of his ministry to the Bishop, during divine service, and as an indication that his chief duty is to look after the cleanliness of the altar and the Table of Oblations.

Note 2.—THE PROMOTION to a higher rank in the hierarchy of an arch-deacon, an arch-priest, an *hegumen*, (Father Superior of a monastery), and an archimandrite takes place during the Liturgy, just before the Introit with the Testament. The candidate for promotion is conducted to the Ambo in the middle of the church, where the Bishop is at the time. The Bishop blesses him, prays that the Lord may, "clothe him with grace, adorn him with righteousness, and grant that he may be a good ensample unto the others;" then, blessing him again, announces to which grade he promotes him and calls out, "*Axios!*" An *hegumen* and an archimandrite are presented with a pastoral staff, and the archimandrite is, besides, invested with the mitre and the pectoral cross.

THE ORDER OF THE SACRAMENT OF MATRIMONY.

Matrimony is the Sacrament, in which, in the image of the union of Christ with the Church, the conjugal union between a man and woman is blessed, which means that the grace of a love as perfect as that which unites Christ and his Church is invoked on them for the blessed bearing and Christian rearing of children.

As matrimony can be entered into only by the mutual spontaneous consent of both the parties, and they must receive the blessing of the Church on their conjugal life, the order of the Sacrament of Matrimony consists of two rites—that of betrothal and that of marriage. In the former the man and the woman affirm their mutual engagement before God and the Church; the rings are the pledge of that engagement. In the rite of marriage their union is blessed with prayers, invoking upon them the grace of the Holy Ghost; of that grace the crowns are the visible token. In ancient times it was allowed to perform the rite of betrothal apart from that of marriage. In our day the latter is performed immediately after the former. Both these rites must be performed in a church, in the presence of witnesses, and on certain days prescribed by the canons.

Note.—The mutual consent of a man and a woman to enter into matrimony is first made known in the home, to a circle of relatives and acquaintances. On this occasion it is customary to have a Te-Deum sung, for the prosperous completion of the matter undertaken, the betrothal rings are given to the engaged couple, in token of consent to their marriage, and their parents or elders bless them with ikons of the Savior and His Mother. The Te-Deum with the ceremonies of giving the rings and blessing constitute what is usually called " betrothal." But a home betrothal cannot take the place of the betrothal in church, which must all the same be performed immediately before the rite of marriage. The home betrothal is a family matter; the promise is made only before relatives and intimates. In the church betrothal this promise is affirmed before the entire church.

The Rite of Betrothal.—The priest, preceded by a lampadary, comes out of the Sanctuary through the Royal Gates holding in his hands the cross and Testament, which he lays on a lectern in the middle of the church. Then he approaches the main entrance of the church, where the bride and groom already stand (the former at the groom's left side), blesses them thrice with two lighted candles, which he then hands to them, conducts them into the church, walking before them and swinging the censer—the censing is expressly prescribed—and places them before the lectern, at a little distance from it. The betrothal begins with the Great Ectenia and two brief prayers, with the addition of special petitions: for the salvation of the betrothed couple, the granting them of children and peaceful mutual affection, for their abiding in harmony, firm in the faith, and for a blessing on them, that they may lead a blameless life. The prayers contain petitions for a blessing on the betrothed and on the betrothal. Then follows the ceremony of betrothal. The priest takes from the altar the rings which he received from the bride and groom before the beginning of the service. With the golden ring he makes the sign of the cross thrice above the groom's head, with the words: "The servant of God N. is betrothed to the handmaid of God N. in the name of the Father, and the Son, and the Holy Ghost." This he repeats thrice, then slips the ring on the fourth finger (next to the little finger) of the groom's right hand. The same proceeding is repeated with the bride's silver ring. After the betrothal, it is prescribed by the canons of the Church that the sponsor, or, as is now the established custom, the groom's best man, shall change the rings thrice from one to the other, so that the bride's silver ring remains with the groom, and the groom's golden ring remains with the bride. The rings are given them in token of the lifelong union into which they are entering.* The more precious metal of the groom's ring indicates his domination, while the exchange of rings between the bride and groom indicates that they engage to share all the toils and hardships of life, he not allowing himself to be uplifted by his supremacy, she not taking advantage of her weakness. That this exchange is made by the sponsor, generally selected among the elder relatives, indicates the consent of the family. The rite of betrothal ends with the priest praying "that the Lord may stablish these espousals in the faith, in harmony, truth and love, and may bless from Heaven this putting on of rings."

---

*In ancient times rings were used as seals, with which to seal storerooms in houses; so the possession of the master's ring gave power in the household. Consequently the exchange of rings meant mutual support and common power over the household.

The Rite of Marriage.—After the rite of betrothal the bride and groom approach nearer to the lectern, holding the lighted candles, and again preceded by the censing priest. This serves to remind them that they must live their lives in conformity with the commandments of the Lord, which the priest proclaims, that their good deeds must shine in the world, and rise to Heaven like incense. As they approach, Psalm 127th is sung, in which are depicted the blessings which God sends to pious consorts:—" Blessed is every one that feareth the Lord; that walketh in His ways.—For thou shalt eat the labor of thine hands; happy shalt thou be, and it shall be well with thee.—Thy wife shall be as a fruitful vine by the sides of thine house; thy children like olive plants round about thy board.—Behold, thus shall the man be blessed, that feareth the Lord.—The Lord shall bless thee out of Zion; and thou shalt see the good of Jerusalem all the days of thy life.—Yea, thou shalt see thy children's children: peace be upon Israel!"—This psalm is sung with the refrain after each verse: " Glory to Thee, our God, glory to Thee." The betrothed couple, in token of festivity, then take their stand on a rug. The priest now asks them, each separately, whether they have the spontaneous wish and firm intention to contract the conjugal union with each other, and whether they have not promised to contract that union with any one else. On receiving their affirmative answer to the former question and their negative to the second, the priest proceeds to the actual rite of marriage.

This rite begins with blessing the Kingdom of the Most Holy Trinity and with the Great Ectenia. To this Ectenia are added petitions on behalf of the new consorts: that they be granted a blessing upon their marriage, chastity, well-favoured children and joy in them, and a blameless life. Then the priest says three prayers, in which he asks that the Lord may grant to the consorts a peaceful life, length of days, chastity, mutual love, long life to their children, grace in their offspring, an unfading crown of glory in the heavens, and an abundance of the good things of the earth so that they may be enabled to assist the needy;—that the Lord may help the wife to obey her husband, and the husband to be the head of his wife; that He may remember also the parents who reared them, as parents' prayers make firm the foundations of houses. After these prayers the priest places a crown on the head of the groom, repeating thrice the words: "The servant of God N. is crowned for the handmaid of God N. in the name of the Father and the Son and the Holy Ghost." This he repeats, placing the other crown on the head of the bride, after which he blesses them thrice, saying "O Lord, our God, with glory and honor crown them." The crowns betoken their victory over their passions, as also the honor paid them for the chastity of their life before marriage, and reminds them that they must guard the purity of their lives after marriage also. In Greece they use wreaths of myrtle and olive branches. We in Russia use crowns in the shape of imperial ones, ornamented with images of the Savior and His Mother. This indicates that the newly wedded spouses are to become the progenitors (*Kniaz* in the old language), of a new generation.

After the ceremony of marriage and the blessing, a Prokimenon is sung, in which the essence of the Sacrament of Matrimony is set forth: "Thou hast set upon their heads crowns of precious stones; they asked life of Thee, and Thou gavest it them," after which Lessons from the Gospels and Epistle are read. The Epistle Lesson speaks of the importance of the Sacrament of Matrimony and of the mutual duties of the consorts; the Gospel Lesson tells of Christ's presence at the wedding at Cana in Galilee.

The readings are followed by the Triple Ectenia and the Ectenia of Supplication, ending with the chanting of the Lord's Prayer; then a cup with wine is brought. The priest blesses the cup, and presents it alternately to the husband and the wife to drink from, three times to each. This common cup signifies that they must live in an indissoluble union and share with each other joy and sorrow. The priest takes them by the hand and leads them three times around the lectern, while the sponsors (or, in Russia, the best men), follow holding the crowns above their heads. During this circumambulation the same hymns are sung as at an ordination.* This ceremony is symbolical of the solemnity and indissolubility of the conjugal union.

The priest now takes the crowns from the newly married couple, and addresses to each words of greeting and good wishes. To the husband he says: " Be thou magnified, O bridegroom, like Abraham, and blessed like Isaac, and increase like Jacob, walking in peace and performing in righteousness the commandments of God." To the bride he says as he takes off her crown: " And thou, O bride, be magnified like Sarah, and rejoice like Rebecca, and increase like Rachel, being glad in thy husband and keeping the bounds of the law, for so is God well-pleased." The couple, after the crowns have been removed, bow their heads at the priest's invitation, listen to his wishes of prosperity and give each other the kiss of love.

In ancient times newly wedded couples used to wear wreaths of myrtle or olive branches for the space of seven days, and on the eighth removed them in church in the presence of the priest, who prayed to God to preserve their union inviolate. In our day this prayer is said immediately after the ceremony, before dismissal.

Conditions of the Legality of a Marriage.—Besides the mutual consent of the parties, the following conditions must be observed for a marriage to be legal: 1) they must be of the legal age—the groom not less then 18, the bride not less than 16;—2) they must not be nearly related. The forbidden relationship extends to the fourth degree, *i. e.* first cousins may not marry

---

*The *first* hymn celebrates the Incarnation of Emmanuel and praises the Mother of God. In the *second* the crowned martyrs are besought to pray for the salvation of our souls, as a warning to the new consorts that they may walk through life in holiness and courageously overcome all temptations and allurements. The *third* hymn glorifies Christ, the Apostles' boast and Martyrs' joy, at the same time indicating that to the consorts also Christ should be their glory and joy in times of affliction, such as they are sure to encounter and share together in the course of their lives.

each other, nor may two brothers marry two sisters; within the fifth degree (the father's or mother's first cousin), and the sixth (second cousins), marriage is sometimes permitted, but not without a dispensation from the Bishop;—3) both parties must be of sane mind, and 4) must have authority to marry: if minors, from parents or guardians;—if employed in military or civil service, from their superiors;—if members of a commune, from the elder. In order to find out whether there are any obstacles to the projected marriage, the bans are published in the couple's parish church for three consecutive feast-days. In addition to this, information is procured concerning their age, their families, their religion, whether they are not already married to some other person,—unmarried or widowed, and, if the latter, after having been married once or more than once, lastly, whether they have the necessary authority from parents, guardians or superiors. All this information is entered into a book; the entry is then signed by the groom and bride, and by witnesses who certify the truth of the information and engage, in case their testimony should be proved false, to answer before the laws, civil and ecclesiastical. This is called the "record," and not until it is completed and signed, can the marriage ceremonies be performed.

The Order for a Second Marriage.—The Orthodox Church allows widowers and widows, and also persons whose marriage has been dissolved for one of the legitimate reasons, to contract a second and a third marriage; but this she considers as a condescension to human weakness, and therefore the celebration of a second or third marriage does not take place with the same solemnity as that of a first marriage. The prayers at the rites of betrothal are omitted, and those that accompany the rite of marriage are of a penitential nature; the solemn entrance of the bridal pair to the singing of the 127th Psalm is also omitted. In ancient times crowns were not used. It is customary in our day to limit these curtailed rites to the cases when both parties have been married before. Where one of the two is contracting a first marriage, the rites are not curtailed.

THE SACRAMENT OF EXTREME UNCTION.

Extreme Unction is the Sacrament in the administration of which a sick person is anointed with holy oil, while the grace of the Holy Ghost is invoked on him, which healeth sickness, both bodily and spiritual. The oil for this Sacrament is consecrated by prayer, and it should be, according to the canons of the Church, performed by seven priests; but in case of need, one priest suffices.

A dish with wheat is placed upon a table. Into the midst of the wheat is placed a vessel containing oil and red wine, and around the dish are fastened seven candles and seven bodkins or twigs like that used in the rites of baptism and confirmation, wrapped around with cotton. Upon the same table are placed a cross and Testament. The grains of wheat symbolize resurrection and regeneration;* the oil—healing by the grace of God, and the red wine, mixed with the oil, indicate that the grace of God is given us for Christ's sake, who shed His blood on the cross for our salvation. The seven candles symbolize the seven gifts of the Holy Ghost. During the performance of the sacramental rites the patient and the by-standers hold in their hands lighted candles.

The service begins with the singing of prayers for the healing of the patient. It consists principally of a canon which is sung with the refrain: " O Lord of many mercies, heal thy suffering servant!" Then the Great Ectenia is recited, with added petitions for the blessing of the oil by the descent of the Holy Ghost, and for the granting to the sufferer of the grace of the Holy Ghost. After this the priest prays that the Lord may sanctify this oil, so that it may be to those anointed with it for healing and deliverance from all passion, all defilement of flesh and spirit and from all evil.

---

*The grain, though dry, carries in itself the vital germ of a new plant; thus a sick man may recover, though dried up by disease, if so it please God. The grain, when laid in the earth, rots, yet its vital principle revives in a new plant; thus he who dies of sickness, though given to corruption in the earth, will in due time arise to new life.

The consecration of the oil is followed by the reading of seven Lessons from the Epistle, seven from the Gospels, the Triple Ectenia, seven times repeated, seven prayers for the healing of the sick man and the remission of his sins, lastly anointments of his body with the consecrated oil. After each Lesson from the Epistle and from the Gospel, and the Ectenia, one of the priests, with a prayer for the recovery of the patient, takes up one of the bodkins, dips it in the oil and wine, and anoints him crosswise on the forehead, nostrils, cheeks, lips, breast and hands, uttering the while the sacramental words:—" Holy Father, physician of souls and bodies, do Thou heal thy servant N. of the spiritual and bodily infirmities which possess him and quicken him with the grace of Thy Christ." After the seventh anointment, the patient rises up and stands in the midst of the priests, or, if he is unable to rise, the priests come and stand around his bed. Then the senior priest takes the Testament, opens and holds it, text downward, as it were Christ's own hand, upon the patient's head and recites a prayer for the remission of his sins. The patient kisses the Testament, and, after hearing the dismissal, asks a blessing of the priests: " Bless, holy fathers, me, a sinner."

The Sacrament of Extreme Unction is administered to persons suffering from severe illness; but it is not necessary that the patient should have reached utter exhaustion or unconsciouness. This Sacrament may be administered more than once. One to whom health has been restored after receiving Extreme Unction is not pledged thereby to renounce the world, to take monastic vows and to devote the rest of his days to perpetual penance and fasting.

Note.—EXTREME UNCTION PUBLICLY ADMINISTERED ON THURSDAY OF THE HOLY WEEK.—In the Church of the Assumption, at Moscow, on Holy Thursday before the Liturgy, a bishop administers Extreme Unction to persons healthy in body, but morally suffering from spleen, despondency, and desirous of receiving it in view of the uncertainty of the hour of death. The Bishop consecrates the oil and pours some red wine into it. Then follows the reading of Lessons from the Epistle and the Gospels. Of the prayers only the seventh is recited. After that the Bishop stirs the oil and wine with the sacramental spoon, pours out the mixture into small vessels, then anoints on the forehead first himself, the priests and deacons and distributes the vessels among the priests, who anoint the people. When this is done, the Bishop recites the prayer for the remission of sins, while the priests hold over his head the open Testament, text downward.

TE-DEUMS.

A Te-Deum is a special service, in which prayers of thanksgiving and petition are offered to the Lord, to the Mother of God and the Saints, on occasion of some special occurrence in the life of the nation or of individuals.

Te-Deums belong either to public or to private worship. Under the head of "public worship" come Te-Deums performed: 1.) on "imperial anniversaries," *i. e.* on the birthdays and names' days of members of the Imperial House, on the day of the accession to the throne of the reigning Emperor, the day of the Coronation of their Imperial Majesties;—2) on the day of a temple-feast, *i. e.* the day sacred to the commemoration of the person or event in whose name and honor a given parish church has been named and dedicated;—3) on "victorial anniversaries," i. e. days commemorating victories over enemies;—4) on occasions of public calamities, such as foreign invasion, epidemics, pestilence, drought or excessive rains, and the like. To "private worship" belong Te-Deums performed at the desire of private persons on their birthdays and name's days, before children begin lessons, when any one starts on a journey, when a new dwelling is entered, when thanks are given for some mercy which had been prayed for, for the recovery of a sick person, etc., etc.

Te-Deums are of three kinds: one includes the singing of a Canon, another omits the Canon, and the third omits the Gospel Lesson.

The Order of the Te-Deums With Canon is as follows: After the preliminary exclamation by the priest, "O Heavenly King..." is sung, then the Trisagion and the Lord's Prayer; after that a psalm is read, selected with reference to the object prayed for. After the psalm the Great Ectenia is recited, with the addition of petitions bearing on the occasion of the Te-Deum. Then are sung: " God is the Lord..", Troparia and the Penitential Psalm " Have mercy on me, O Lord " (*Miserere*) and at last the Canon with refrains in the honor of the person invoked; for instance, in a Canon to the Holy Trinity, the refrain is " Most Holy Trinity, our God, glory to Thee;" in a Canon to the Virgin it is " Most holy Mother of God, save us;" in a Canon to St. Nicholas—" Father and Bishop Nicholas, pray God for us."

After the third Ode of the Canon the Triple Ectenia is recited; after the sixth Ode the Little Ectenia, which is followed by a Lesson from the Gospels (if the Te-Deum is in honor of two or more Saints, two or more Lessons are read); after the ninth Ode the hymn " Meet and right..." is sung. This is followed by the Trisagion, the Lord's Prayer, and the Triple Ectenia, after which a special prayer is read, appropriate to the object of petition or thanksgiving. Thus a Te-Deum with Canon is, in its order, an abbreviation of Matins. An Akathistos is sometimes joined with the Canon, when it is recited after the sixth Ode, before the Gospel Lesson. Te-Deums with Canons are sung on temple-feasts in honor of the Lord and His Saints, for deliverance from foes, in times of excessive rain, drought or epidemic.

The Te-Deum without Canon proceeds in the same manner until the hymn " God is the Lord." After that and the Troparia, Lessons from the Epistle and Gospels are read (sometimes a Parœmia is read before the Epistle Lesson); the Gospel Lesson is followed by the Triple Ectenia, after which the priest recites the special prayer for the occasion, which is listened to kneeling, and the Great Doxology is sung. Sometimes a prayer for the granting of length of days to the Emperor and his House is said after the Doxology. Te-Deums of this kind are sung on New Year's Day, on the anniversary of the reigning Emperor's accession to the throne and of the Coronation, to give thanks for some great mercy, for the safety of the Emperor and the soldiers in battle, on occasion of a child's first lesson, for recovery from sickness, to ask a blessing on those that depart on journeys or to "navigate the waters" and on bee-hives.

There is no Gospel Lesson when the object of the Te-Deum is to ask a blessing on various inanimate objects; such as a war-vessel, an army flag, arms or ordnance, a new ship or boat,—or on the digging of a well or finding of water, or a newly completed well. All such articles are besprinkled with holy water; hence to Te-Deums is joined the rite of the Lesser Consecration of water, which is performed after the model of the consecration prescribed for the 1st of August.

THE ORDER OF THE CONSECRATION OF A MONK.

The name of *Monk* is given to persons who have taken the vows of chastity, poverty, and absolute obedience to the will of their spiritual guides, with complete surrender of their own will. Monks live together in separate buildings, called *Monasteries* or *Lauras*. There each monk has a place to himself, which is called a *cell*.* They assemble all together only in the church, for services, in the refectory, and at their common work. They are all in perfect subordination to the will of their chief, the Father Superior of the monastery, who has the title of *Hegumen* (a Greek word which means "leader"), or of *Archimandrite* (another Greek word which means "chief of a fold"). At the present time all Hegumens and Archimandrites have the dignity of priesthood; but this was not always the case in ancient times. Monks are divided into three grades: that of *novices, monks of the lesser vows* and *of the highest vows*. Persons who desire to take on themselves monastic vows, do not at once enter the ranks of monks; they are first subjected to tests, to prove the firmness of their intent. In other words they pass through the "ordeal of obedience," sometimes lasting several years, during which they are on probation, and therefore are called *probationers* or *lay brethren*. Both these and the

---

*A *Laura* is a large monastery, with a great number of inmates. A *Cell* is literally, a cellar, a store-room, a small chamber.

novices are under the special guidance of an older monk, of their own choice, who is called an *ancient*. As one of the acts of a monk's consecration consists in cutting or *tonsuring* his hair, the ceremony is also called *tonsure*. There is a special order of consecration for every grade of monastic life.

The Order of Investing With the Robe.—After the prefatory prayers and penitential Troparia, the Hegumen recites a prayer wherein he asks the Lord to vouchsafe that the probationer who desires to enter monastic life may acquit himself worthily in the *angelic state** and to admit him into the flock of His elect; then he tonsures the hair on the novice's head in the form of a cross, " in the name of the Father, and the Son, and the Holy Ghost," in token that he, the novice, " casts from him all idle thoughts and acts and takes upon himself the yoke of the Lord." After the tonsuring, the Hegumen invests him with the garb of his order, the *robe (riássa)* and the *kamilávka* or skull-cap, both black and of inexpensive material. The robe is a wide garment, unbelted, such as was worn in ancient times on days of sorrowing; the monk dons it in token of grief for his sins; while the *kamilávka* (the word means *a cap protecting from the heat*, or *allaying heat*) betokens the taming of the passions. By assuming the robe, the probationer enters the ranks of the " newly-consecrated " or novices, and receives the title of *riassophor*, i. e., " wearer of the robe," but takes no vows.

The Order of the Lesser Schema.—The word *Schema* means " dignity, aspect;" the " Order of the Lesser Schema " is the name given to the consecration of a novice into the second grade of monastic life, that of monk proper. This rite generally takes place in church, before the Liturgy or after Matins. The novice who wishes to take the vows removes his garments on the porch, in token that he renounces all wrong-doing, and stands unbelted, unshod, and bareheaded. Then the brethren (i. e., the community of the monastery) come

---

*The monastic state is called " angelic " because monks take the vow of renunciation of all things worldly, do not marry, do not acquire or hold property, and live as the angels do in heaven, glorifying God night and day and striving to do His will in all things.

forth from the church to fetch him, with lighted candles, chanting a Troparion which celebrates the return of the prodigal son to his father's house, and conduct him into the church. The

MONASTIC GARMENTS.

1. The Robe (*Riássa*).
2. The Chaplet.
3. The *Klobuk*.
4. The Mantle or Pallium.
5. The Cowl (*Cucullus*).
6. Bishop's Mantle.
7. The Belt.
8. The *Analavon*.
9. The *Paramand*.

novice performs three prostrations on the way, stops opposite the Royal Gates, before a lectern on which are laid a cross and Testament, and here, to the question of the Hegumen, who asks him "what he seeks in coming hither?" replies "I seek a life of mortification." Then the Hegumen questions him further: "Whether he aspires to the angelic state? Whether he gives himself to God of his own free will? Whether he intends to abide in the monastery and lead a life of mortification unto his latest breath? Whether he intends to keep himself in the observance of virginity, chastity and piety? Whether he will remain obedient to the superior and to the brethren unto death? Whether he will endure willingly the restraint and hardships of monastic life?" When he has answered to all these questions "Yea, reverend Father, with the help of God,"—the Hegumen explains to him wherein monastic life consists. He pledges himself to keep his vows. Then the Hegumen prays that "the Lord may receive him, shield him by the operation of the Holy Ghost and deliver him from all carnal lusts," and, laying his hand on the Testament adds: "Here Christ is present invisibly. Behold! no one compels thee to come to Him." Then, the better to test his willingness to take the vows, he hands him the shears thrice, with the words: "Take these shears and give them to me." The novice every time receives the shears and returns them to the Hegumen, kissing his hand. After the third time the Hegumen says to him: "From the hand of Christ thou didst receive them. Behold to Whom thou joinest thyself, Whom thou embracest, and whom thou renouncest." Then the Hegumen tonsures the novice's head in the form of a cross saying: "Our brother (or our sister) cuts the hair of his (or her) head in the name of the Father, and the Son, and the Holy Ghost," and in doing so changes his (or her) name for another, in token of complete renunciation of the world* and perfect self-consecration to God.

The recipient of the Schema is now invested with the garb of his order. He dons a *chiton*, usually called *tunic* or *cassock*, as an emblem of poverty; in ancient times this tunic was made of horsehair; then he puts on an article called *paramand*, which

---

*Hence it is customary to give to monks names which are used seldom or not at all among laymen.

means "something besides, or added to the mantle." This name is given to a square of cloth, on which is represented the cross of Christ with the lance, the reed, and the inscription: "*I wear upon my body the wounds of my Lord.*" By means of strings sewed to the corners, this square is fastened around the shoulders and waist of the monk. It is intended to remind him that he has taken on himself the yoke of Christ and must control his passions and desires. At the same time a cross is hung on his neck, in token that he is to follow Christ. Over these the monk puts on the robe, which is now called "the robe of rejoicing," and girds himself with the belt, in token of spiritual regeneration and mortification of the body. Over the robe the monk is invested with the *pallium* or *mantle,* a wide garment, very long and without sleeves. It is called "the garment of incorruption and purity," and the absence of sleeves is to remind the monk that he is debarred from worldly pursuits. The mantle is given him in token of the "exalted angelic state" which he assumes, *i. e.,* as a pledge that he will not stop on this second grade, but will seek the third, highest. The head-gear given to him is the *kamilávka* with the *klobúk* or *veil,* which is to remind him that he must veil his face from temptation, and guard his eyes and ears against all vanity.* Therefore the *klobúk* is called the "helmet of salvation." The feet of the monk are shod with *sandals* (shoes), in token that he should abide in peace and calm, and be slow in pursuing his own wishes or doing his own will. Lastly he is given a *chaplet,* i. e., a cord with many knots, to count prayers and prostrations by. This chaplet is the monk's spiritual sword, which helps him to conquer absent-mindedness while at prayers, by which he drives evil counsel from his soul. Sometimes the chaplet consists of small metallic plates strung on a string or rope, at equal intervals; it is then called by a name which means "small ladder" (*liéstofka*) because it looks like one.

After the vesting the Great Ectenia is recited, with the addition of special petitions on behalf of the new brother, and the

---

*Cap and veil together are commonly called by the one name, *klobúk.*

Prokimenon is sung: "As many as have been baptized into Christ, have put on Christ;" then Lessons are read—from the Epistle, how that every man must wage war against the foes of Salvation, and invest himself to that end with the full panoply of God—and from the Gospel, how that the love of God must be greater than the love of parents, and how he that does not follow in the footsteps of the Lord is unwothy of Him. Then the new brother is presented with a candle and a cross, and reminded of the words of Christ, that whoever would follow Him must take up his cross, and glorify his Heavenly Father by his good deeds. Lastly the Hegumen and all the brethren give him the kiss of welcome.

The Order of the Great Schema, or Highest Angelic State.—Those monks who take upon themselves the *Great Schema*, are called in Russia *Schemniks*. They take severer vows of complete renunciation of the world. The consecration for this highest grade differs from that of the lesser grade in the following points: 1. The vestments prepared for the candidate are taken into the Sanctuary the evening before, and laid upon the altar, to signify that he receives them from the Lord Himself; 2. his name is again changed at his consecration; 3. in the place of the *paramand*, he puts on the *analavon*, which answers to the *paramand*, but is ornamented with many crosses and worn on the shoulders, to signify the bearing of his cross in following Christ; 4. instead of the flat-topped *klobuk*, he puts on a pointed cap called a *cowl* (*cucullus*), with veil covering the head and shoulders and decorated with five crosses: on the brow, the breast, the shoulders and the back. It is called "the cowl of guilelessness" and "the helmet of hope in salvation."

Consecration of an Hegumen or Archimandrite.—When a monk is consecrated for Hegumen (Father Superior), he is given a *pastoral staff* emblematic of his duty as ruler of the community. If he is consecrated for the dignity of an Archimandrite, he is invested with a mantle which has four squares of red or green cloth called *tables of the law* sewed on in front, at the neck and at the bottom. They signify that the Archimandrite is the monk's instructor and guide in living in accordance with the commandments of God. Bishops, who at the present time are taken from among the Archimandrites, wear mantles, not black, but of some light color with stripes of another color, which begin at the neck and run all around the mantle down to the skirt. These stripes are called "*rivers*" and signify that from the bishop's lips flow rivers of instruction in the Word of God.

THE BURIAL AND COMMEMORATION OF THE DEAD.

The Prayers for a Departing Soul.—The Orthodox Church bestows on the dying a blessing and a parting word to ease their passage into life eternal at the moment of the separation of the soul from the body. This parting word consists of a prayerful Canon to our Lord Jesus Christ and to His Immaculate Mother. The Troparia of this Canon express, on behalf of the dying person, the consciousness of sin, the fear of punishment, and the hope in the intercession of the Mother of God and in the mercy of Christ. The Canon ends with a prayer that the Lord may remit the dying person's sins and grant his soul rest with the saints in the eternal abodes.

The Preparation of a Deceased Christian's Body for Burial.—After death, a Christian's body is washed and clothed in new garments. The latter either are all white, when they are called a *shroud* or *winding-sheet*, and refer to the promise which the deceased gave at baptism to lead a life of purity and holiness,—or else they are the garments of his rank and dignity in life, in token that he must render an account to God of the manner in which he acquitted himself of the duties of the position to which he was called. On his brow is placed a phylactery or band on which are represented Christ, His Mother and John the Baptist, with the words of the Trisagion, in token that the deceased, as a warrior of Christ, contended on earth for the truth and died with the hope of receiving a crown in Heaven. In the hands is placed an ikon of the Savior or of some Saint, symbolizing the deceased's faith in Christ and his wish to be admitted into the community of holy disciples. Then the body is laid in a coffin and covered with a pall, to signify that the deceased is under the shelter of the Church of Christ.

The Reading of the Psalter by the Coffin and the Requiem Services.—Immediately after a Christian's death the reading of the Psalter begins by his coffin, with the addition, after each "Glory" (*stasis* or *antiphon*) of prayers for the rest of his soul, and Requiem services are celebrated, called *pannychida*, which means "an all-night service." But they are in reality only short services, consisting of petitions for the forgiveness of the deceased's sins and the rest of his soul in the Kingdom of Heaven. This service is an abbreviation of Matins. It begins with the reading or chanting of Psalm 90: "He that dwelleth in the defence of the Most High, shall abide under the shelter of the Almighty." . . . Then follows the Great Ectenia, with an added petition for the departed, after which are sung: "Alleluia," Troparia with the refrain "Blessed Art Thou, O Lord," the Penitential Psalm, the Canon with three Little Ectenias after the third, sixth and ninth Odes, the Trisagion, the Lord's Prayer, funeral Troparia, the Triple Ectenia, and Dismissal, proclaiming "Eternal Remembrance" of the departed. During the Requiem the coffin is censed all around, to signify that the soul of the departed, like unto the fumes from the censer, ascendeth to heaven and that our prayers for him are pleasing to God. This service bears the name of an "all-night service," because, in ancient times, at the funeral of martyrs, the Christians used to spend the entire night chanting and praying.

The Bearing forth of the Body to the Church.—The body is taken to a church before burial. Just before it is borne forth from the house, a short service, called *Litê* is held,—an abbreviated Requiem—consisting of Troparia, the Triple Ectenia and Dismissal. The coffin is again censed all around during this service. The body of the departed brother is carried to the church to the chanting of the Trisagion in token that the departed now passeth into the abode of the celestial hosts, there to sing with them the hymn to the Holy Trinity. The Christians who surround the coffin hold lighted candles in their hands, thereby expressing the certainty that their departed brother ascendeth into eternal light, which is God. The coffin is placed in the middle of the church, facing the Sanctuary, and lights are lit all around it.

The Funeral Service.—The entire funeral rite is inspired by prayer for the departed and the desire to console the survivors. It begins with the chanting of Psalms 90 and 118, which set forth the blessedness of them that have lived trusting in the help of the Most High and in the observance of His law. Then, after "Alleluia" has been sung thrice, follow Troparia with the refrain "Blessed art Thou, O Lord; teach me Thy justifications." In these Troparia man's entire lot is pictured. Created from nothing, but endowed with the likeness of God, he returns to earth for having transgressed the divine commandment; yet, nothwithstanding that he bears upon him the ulcers of sin, he still retains the image of the ineffable glory of God, and dares to beseech the merciful Lord for restoration to his glorious home. The Troparia are followed by the singing of the funeral Canon, containing prayers for the departed; after the third, sixth and ninth Odes, the Little Ectenia is recited. Then are sung the *Idiomela*: these are eight Stichera, which contain the lamentations of man who realizes how fleeting and perishable are earthly things. Each Stichera is sung to a tone or melody of its own (as indicated by the name).

"What sweet of life abideth unaccompanied with grief? What glory stayeth on earth unalterable? All things are feeblest shadows, all are delusive dreams. . . . Where is the predilection of the world? Where are the imaginings of them who themselves are fleeting? Where is the silver and the gold? Where the multitude of servants and the renown? . . . All dust, all ashes, all a shadow! . . . I weep and lament when I see our comeliness, created in the likeness of God, lying in graves disfigured, bereft of glory and of form. O wonder! what is this mystery concerning us? how have we been given over to corruption? how to death conjoined? Verily, by the command of God, as it is written, Who giveth the departed rest."

After the Idiomela the Beatitudes are chanted; then are read Lessons from the Epistle and Gospel, which speak of the resurrection of the dead, and give comfort to them that mourn over the vanity of all earthly things.

The Lessons from Scripture are followed by the Ectenia of Supplication, which concludes with the "prayer of absolution," in which the Church remits all the departed's transgressions, absolves him from all obligations, all pledges or oaths, and sends him off in peace into life everlasting. In token that the prayers of the Church have weight with God and that what is remitted to the penitent on earth is remitted to them in heaven also, it is customary in our country to place in the departed's hands a paper with this prayer written upon it.

The funeral service ends with the singing of Sticheræ, which speak of the separation of our departed brother from us and express his request that we should pray for him. This is the moment when the last kiss is given and the coffin is closed down; then "eternal remembrance" of the departed is proclaimed.

Burial, or Laying the Body in the Grave.—When the funeral service is concluded, the coffin is lowered into the grave, facing the East, to signify that the deceased is going towards the Orient of life everlasting, to await the second coming of Christ, the Sun of Truth. While the coffin is being lowered, the prayers of the Litê are chanted; then the priest casts earth crosswise upon the coffin, saying: "The earth is the Lord's and the fulness thereof, the world and all they that dwell therein," and pours oil upon it, if the departed received extreme unction in life, also scatters on it ashes from the censer. This oil, unused for the lamp, and these extinct ashes symbolize the life which has been extinguished on earth, but, is, by God's mercy, to be resurrected for everlasting bliss.

Christian graves are dug either in a cemetery which surrounds a church, or within the church building, to signify that they who have been true to the Church in life, are sheltered by her in death.

Prayers and Rites After the Burial.—The Church cares for Christians in death. She prays for them and offers the Bloodless Sacrifice of the Liturgy in their behalf on the third, ninth and fortieth day after their decease, then every year on the anniversary of death, which is called the "day of remembrance" or "commemoration." On the third day we pray that Christ, Who rose from the dead on the third day after His death, may resurrect our departed brother into a life of blessedness; on the ninth day we pray the Lord that He may number the departed among the nine orders of Angels and Saints; on the fortieth day we beseech Christ that He, Who endured temptation from the Devil on the fortieth day of His fast, may help the departed to stand the ordeal of God's judgment without being shamed, and that He, Who ascended to Heaven on the fortieth day, may receive the departed into the heavenly abode. Sometimes he is commemorated daily through all the forty days, by the celebration of the Liturgy in memory of him. By devoting to prayer the anniversary day of our brother's demise, we express the belief that the day of a man's death is not the day of his annihilation, but of his birth into life everlasting.

At all commemorative services is set forth a dish of boiled wheat or rice with honey (*Kolivo* or *Kutyà*). The grain symbolizes resurrection, while the honey (or sugar) indicates the sweet, blissful life in the Kingdom of Heaven.

Apart from private commemorations of every deceased Christian, at the wish of his friends and relatives, there are certain days set apart by the Church for the commemoration of all deceased Christians generally. The church services for these days are called "Universal Requiems," and the days themselves are called "ancestral days" (All-Souls'). Such days are: the Saturday before the Butter-week (Carnival); the Saturdays of the second, third and fourth weeks in Lent; the Saturdays before Trinity (Pentecost) and before the feast of St. Dimitri of Thessalonica (26th of October); the Tuesday—in some localities the Monday— of St. Thomas' week (the week after Easter) and the day of the Decollation of John the Baptist. The Saturday before St. Dimitri's feast was instituted in memory of the Great-Prince (*Veliki-Kniaz*) Dimitri Donskoy and of the warriors killed on the Field of Kulikof in the great battle against the Tatars.

Special Features of the Burial of Priests and Babes.— The body of a priest is not washed, but sponged with pure oil and clothed in the sacred vestments. The face is covered with an aër and in the hands are placed a cross and Testament. The body is borne to the church in procession, the church bells ringing a carillon. Before every church which the procession passes the Litê service is performed. During the funeral service five Lessons from the Epistle and five from the Gospels are read; after the funeral Canon the Sticheræ on " Praise the Lord " are sung, then the Great Doxology. More Idiomela are sung than at the funerals of laymen.

For babes who have died after receiving baptism, the funeral service is performed after a special rite, the Church praying, not that the departed's sins be forgiven him, but that the Lord, according to His unfailing promise, may vouchsafe to receive him, as being blessed and undefiled, into the Kingdom of Heaven.

For babes who have died unbaptized, no funeral service is performed, they not having been cleansed of the original sin. Of their future lot St. Gregory the Divine says that they will be neither glorified nor punished by the righteous Judge, as such that have not received the seal, yet are not wicked, and have suffered more than done harm. " For not every one who is not deserving of punishment is therefore deserving of honor; nor is every one who is not deserving of honor, therefore deserving of punishment."

BOOKS CONTAINING THE DIVINE SERVICE.

The Order of divine service, both public and private, is contained in special books, some of which give the daily service, and others the order of the various ministrations.

Under the former head come: the *Book of Offices*, the *Ordinal*, the *Horologion*, the *Oktoëchos*, the *Monthly Menea*, the *Feast-day Menea*, the *Common Menea*, the *Lenten Triodion*, the *Ferial Triodion*, the *Irmologion* and the *Typikon*.

The Book of Offices (*Slujébnik*) contains the unalterable prayers and ceremonies of Matins, Vespers and the Liturgy, performed by the Priest and the Deacon. The Ordinal (*Tchinóvnik*) is the Pontifical Book of Offices, differing from the other in that it contains all the prayers and ceremonies in use at pontifical services; also the Order of Ordination and consecration for all grades and dignities of the church. The Horologion (*Tchasoslóv*) contains the unalterable prayers of the daily services recited and chanted by the Readers and choristers. The Oktoëchos, the Meneæ, the Triodia and the Irmologion contain the changeable prayers and compositions in use in the daily services, namely: the Oktoëchos (which means the " Book of Eight tones ") contains the changeable songs of praise of the weekly cycle of services. The name of the book comes from this—that the services of the entire week are sung in one "tone," and the " tones " are eight in number. In the monthly Menea we find the changeable prayers appointed for each day of the 12 months; it is therefore divided into 12 parts. The Feast-day Menea contains the prayers for the feasts of the Lord, of the Mother of God and of the more honored Saints, selected from the Monthly Menea. In the Common Menea we find the prayers prescribed in the services in honor of all the Saints of the different orders—apostles, martyrs, prelates. The Triodion (which means the " Book of three songs "), contains the changeable prayers for the moveable days of the yearly cycle of services, and, in the number, the so-called *Triodes*, *i. e.* incomplete Canons, consisting of two, three, or four Odes. There are two Triodia: the Lenten, giving the services for Lent and the preparatory weeks thereto, and the Ferial, giving the services from Easter Sunday to the All-Saints' Week. In the Irmologion we find the prayers which are sung,—not read or recited,—at the various services. This book has its name from the fact that it contains among others, the Irmi of the Canons. The Order of the service for each day of the year is given in the book called Typikon, (which means " statute ").

The services performed by private desire are described in the " Book of Needs " (or " of Ministrations "), in the " Order for the Reception into the Church of Members of alien Creeds " and in the Book of Chants.

Some books belong to both private and public worship. Such are the Gospels, the Epistle, and the Psalter. The former two are divided into Lessons, with the indication of the Lesson for each day. The Psalter is divided into Kathismata and " Glories." The Psalter is sometimes printed in one volume with the Horologion. It is then called "A Psalter with Sequence."

There is still another class of books, which contain extracts from other books, and are meant for private home use, such as: the Book of Rules, which tells how to prepare for Communion, and gives the services and prayers required by these rules,—the Books " of collected Akathistoi," and " of collected Canons;"— the " Book of Saints," giving the Troparia and Kondakia for each day, and the " Euchologion " (Prayer Book), complete or abridged.

Table of Contents.

	PAGE.
PRELIMINARY NOTIONS,	3–6
The Nature of Divine Service,	3
The Origin of Divine Service,	—
External Signs Used in Divine Service,	5
THE CHRISTIAN TEMPLE,	6–22
Names of the Various Temples and their Origin,	6
External Appearance of Churches,	8
The Internal Arrangement of Churches,	9
The Sanctuary and its Belongings,	10
The Chapel of the Prothesis and its Belongings,	14
The Vestry and its Belongings,	16
The Nave or Body of the Church,	—
Vestibule and Porch,	20
Appurtenances of Public Divine Service in Churches,	20
Illumination : Lampads, Candelabra and Candlesticks,	20
Bellringing,	22
OF THE PERSONS WHO PERFORM DIVINE SERVICE AND OF THEIR VESTMENTS,	23–32
The Clergy,	23
The Sacred Vestments,	26
The Antiquity of Vestments,	26
The Sticharion or Tunic,	—
The Orarion and the Epitrachelion,	—
The Maniples and Zone, or Belt,	27
The Phelonion or Cope, and the Saccos,	29
The Omophorion,	30
The Mitre, the Skull-cap ("Kamilavka") and the Scuffia,	—
The Epigonation ("Pàlitsa,") and the Thigh-shield ("Nabédrennik")	—
The Pectoral Cross, the Panagía, the Crozier and the "Orlets" ("Eaglet")	31

	PAGE.
ON PUBLIC WORSHIP,	32–10
THE DAILY, WEEKLY AND YEARLY CYCLES OF SERVICES,	32
The Daily Cycle of Services,	33
The Weekly Cycle,	—
The Yearly Cycle,	34
Feasts,	34
The Paschal Feast,	—
Combinations of Daily Services,	36
OF THE DAILY SERVICES,	36
VESPERS,	40
The Beginning of the Service and the Prœmiac (Prefatory or Introductory) Psalm,	40
The Great Ectenia (Suffrages),	—
The Kathisma,	42
The Little Ectenia,	43
The Verses of the Psalm "Lord, I Have Cried," and their Sticheræ,	—
Vesper Introit and Doxology,	44
The Prokimenon,	45
The Parœmiæ,	—
The Triple Ectenia and the Ectenia of Supplication,	46
Conclusion of Vespers,	47
The Litê and the Blessing of the Loaves (Artoklasia),	—
MATINS,	49
"The Six Psalms,"	49
The Great Ectenia, "God is the Lord," and the Kathismata,	—
The Poly-elaion,	50
The Magnification and the Sunday Troparia,	—
The Matutinal Antiphons,	51
The Gospel Lesson,	—
Adoration of the Testament or the Ikon and anointing with Oil,	52
The Scriptural Odes and the Canon,	53
The Psalm of Praise and the Sticheræ on "Praise ye,"	56
The Great Doxology,	—
End of Matins, and Prime (Office of the First Hour),	57

	PAGE.
THE LITURGY,	59
1) The Proskomidé,	60
2) The Liturgy of the Catechumens,	62
Meaning of the Liturgy of the Catechumens, its Component Parts and its Beginning,	—
The Typical Psalms and the Antiphons,	63
The Introit with the Gospel,	64
The Trisagion,	65
The Reading of Lessons from the Epistle and the Gospel,	—
Common Prayers for the Members of the Church and Departure of the Catechumens,	66
3) The Liturgy of the Faithful,	67
What the Liturgy of the Faithful Represents and the Principal Acts which Compose it,	—
A. Preparation of the Elements and the Faithful for the Sacrifice,	68
The Great Introit,	—
Petition for Spiritual Mercies, Exhortation, Love and Peace, and Profession of Faith,	69
Invitation to Attend,	70
B. The Consummation of the Sacrifice,	71
Commemorating the Members of the Church,	—
C. The Preparation for Communion and the Act of Communion,	74
The Preparation of the Faithful for Communion,	—
The Preparation of the Elements for Communion and the Communion of the Celebrants,	—
The Communion of Laymen,	76
The Blessing and the Last Appearance of the Holy Gifts Before the People,	77
D. Conclusion of the Service,	—
Giving Thanks for Communion,	—
Blessing for Going Forth Out of the Church; Prayer Recited off the Ambo; Distribution of Holy Bread, and Dismissal,	78
Days When the Liturgy of St. Basil the Great is Performed and Wherein it Differs from that of St. John Chrysostom,	79
The Typica or Pro-Liturgy Service,	80

	PAGE.
SPECIAL FEATURES OF DIVINE SERVICE ON FEAST-DAYS AND IN FAST-TIME, ...	80–110

IMMOVABLE FEASTS AND FASTS.

THE UNIVERSAL FEAST OF THE EXALTATION OF THE PRECIOUS AND LIFE-GIVING CROSS OF THE LORD, . .	80
THE NATIVITY OF OUR LORD AND SAVIOR JESUS CHRIST, .	82
THE BAPTISM OF OUR LORD AND SAVIOR JESUS CHRIST, .	84
THE ANNUNCIATION, ...	86
THE DAY OF THE HOLY AND MOST GLORIOUS APOSTLES PETER AND PAUL, ...	87
THE ASSUMPTION OF THE MOTHER OF GOD, ...	88
THE DECOLLATION OF THE HONORABLE GLORIOUS PROPHET AND PRECURSOR, JOHN THE BAPTIST, ...	—
THE BRINGING FORTH OF THE HOLY AND LIFE-GIVING CROSS, ...	89

MOVABLE FEASTS AND FASTS.

THE WEEKS OF PREPARATION FOR LENT, . . .	90
PECULIARITIES OF LENTEN SERVICES, ...	92
The Lenten Hours, ...	93
The Liturgy of the Pre-Sanctified, ...	—
SPECIAL FEATURES OF THE SERVICES IN EACH WEEK OF THE QUADRAGESIMA, ...	96
SPECIAL FEATURES OF THE SERVICES ON THE SABBATH OF LAZARUS AND PALM SUNDAY, ...	98
SPECIAL FEATURES OF THE SERVICES ON THE FIRST THREE DAYS OF PASSION WEEK, ...	99
SPECIAL FEATURES OF THE SERVICE ON HOLY THURSDAY,	100
SPECIAL FEATURES OF THE SERVICE ON GOOD FRIDAY, .	103
SPECIAL FEATURES OF THE SERVICE ON HOLY SATURDAY, .	104
SPECIAL FEATURES OF THE SERVICE ON THE DAY OF THE HOLY PASCHA, ...	106
SPECIAL FEATURES OF THE SERVICES FROM THE PASCHAL WEEK TO ALL-SAINTS' WEEK, ...	108

	PAGE.

OF THE DIFFERENT MINISTRATIONS, . . . 110–158

  ADMINISTERING THE SACRAMENTS OF BAPTISM AND CONFIRMATION.

    Baptism, ... 110
    Confirmation, ... —
    Prayer for a Woman who hath given birth to a child
      and giving a Name to the Child, ... 111
    Prayer on the Fortieth Day after Birth, . . . 112
    The Rite of Reception among the Catechumens, . —
    The Order of Baptism and Confirmation, . . . 114
    The Rites of Ablution and Tonsure, . . . 118
    The Rite of Joining the Church, ... 119
    The Rite of Admission into the Orthodox Church of
      Followers of other Confessions, ... 120

THE RITE OF ANOINTING TSARS AT THEIR CORONATION, . —

THE ORDER OF THE CONSECRATION OF A CHURCH, . . 124
    Rite at the Laying of the Foundation of a Church, 125
    The Rite of the Consecration of a Church, . . 126

THE RITE OF CONFESSION, ... 130

THE RITE OF THE SACRAMENT OF ORDERS, . . . 132
    The Ordering of a Deacon, ... —
    The Ordering of a Presbyter, ... 134
    The Ordering of a Bishop, ... 135

THE ORDER OF THE SACRAMENT OF MATRIMONY, . . . 136
    Matrimony, ... —
    The Rite of Betrothal, ... 137
    The Rite of Marriage, ... 139
    Conditions of the Legality of a Marriage, . . . 141
    The Order for a Second Marriage, ... 142

THE SACRAMENT OF EXTREME UNCTION, ... 143

TE-DEUMS, ... 145
    The Order of Te-Deums with Canon, . . . —
    The Te-Deum without Canon, ... 146

THE ORDER OF THE CONSECRATION OF A MONK, . . . 147
    The Order of Investing with the Robe, . . . 148
    The Order of the Lesser Schema, ... —
    The Order of the Great Schema, or Highest Angelic
      State, ... 152
    Consecration of an Hegumen or Archimandrite, . —

	PAGE.
THE BURIAL AND COMMEMORATION OF THE DEAD,	153
The Prayers for a Departing Soul,	—
The Preparation of a Deceased Christian for Burial,	—
The Reading of the Psalter by the Coffin and the Requiem Services,	154
The Bearing Forth of the Body to the Church,	—
The Funeral Service,	155
Burial, or Laying the Body in the Grave,	156
Prayers and Rites after the Burial,	157
Special Features of the Burial of Priests and Babes,	158
BOOKS CONTAINING THE DIVINE SERVICES,	158–160

www.ingramcontent.com/pod-product-compliance
Lightning Source LLC
Chambersburg PA
CBHW030242170426
43202CB00009B/595